Celebrate!

A sourcebook of children's parties and family traditions by the parents & teachers of First United Nursery School.

Follow Alex, Jacob, Jessica, Mark and Megan throughout a year of celebrations.

Rainbow Publishing Co.
First United Church Nursery School
848 W. Lake Street
Oak Park, Illinois 60301

First Printing February 1987
ISBN 0-9616693-3-0
Printed in the United States of America, by LithoTech, Oak Park, Illinois

Acknowledgments

Celebrate! is the work of many heads, many hearts and many hands. Dawn Fend designed the book and watched over it while it was in production. Audrey Brown, Ann Malone, and Joy Michel provided the illustrations, and Dorothy Borders did the layout. Ideas were developed and tested by Helen Balch, Marilyn Cantisano, Judy Chrisman, Joan Fadden, Jeanette Peters, Pam Todd, Joan White and Wendy Will.

Joan Fadden and Pam Todd wrote the book, Jeanne Williams typed it, and Mary Ziegler edited it. David Strom, Jerry Sebesta, Margaret Rice, Ann Mertz, and Gerry Puncochar raised the funds for publishing. Marketing the finished product was the responsibility of Patty Plattenberger and Ruth Rowe.

Everything else, and there was a good deal of that, was done by Joan White who provided not only a wealth of ideas, experience, and energy, but also a persistent belief in the project.

Thanks are due to our families, whose tolerance is inestimable, to the people of First United Church who supported us, and most of all to the children who shared the joy of testing these parties with us. We hope you enjoy your celebrations as much as we have. Our only regret is that we can't be there to share them with you.

4

Table of Contents

6

Introduction

This is a book about celebrating with children, the book we wished that someone had written when we began our careers as parents, givers of birthday and holiday parties and upholders of family tradition. It is, in fact, a whole shelf of books since it includes not only complete party plans for birthdays and major holidays, but also a multitude of exciting ideas for seasonal celebrations, pet and new baby parties, neighborhood gatherings and spontaneous occasions. The book also offers a variety of ideas for family traditions that can make your celebrations more memorable and meaningful for everyone. Party descriptions suggest experiences in art, music, drama and science, tried and true recipes, invitation ideas, books to read and games to play. Best of all, every idea has been tested and retested by real children and their sometimes painfully real parents.

Knowing how busy you are, we've designed the book so you can spend less time planning and organizing and more time having fun. Each party is a complete unit in itself. You won't need to flip from section to section to find the games, invitations and food you need to put a party together. But you can, if you prefer, use *Celebrate* as a resource, drawing ideas from different parties to create something new.

Many families miss out on the fun of creating their own celebrations because they're unnecessarily intimidated by the prospect of giving a party or are afraid they don't have time for all the preparations involved. Children's parties and family get-togethers don't have to be exhausting or overwhelming. No matter what talents and experience you and your child bring to the task, you'll find here the ideas and confidence you need to create celebrations that are as much fun to prepare for as they are to participate in.

This book rose out of our own love of celebration and our conviction that we don't have to settle for holidays that are glossy, pre-packaged, commercialized and lacking in meaning. That conviction has guided us all the way through the book in our emphasis on homemade invitations and decorations, non-competitive games, nutritious foods, self-expression, conservation of materials and encouragement of a close relationship to nature. An essential part of our philosophy is the belief that celebrating is something you do *with* children, not *for* them. Even young children can and should be equal participants in cooking, planning, and making, but we must remember to suspend judgment, put aside unrealistic expectations of perfection and share their delight in both process and product.

Celebration is something that happens inside as well as outside, an attitude as much as an occasion, and a response to life. If we reclaim our power of choice in how we celebrate, we can make important moments in our lives a source of love, affirmation, and joy in both our own uniqueness and our ties to others. It may be that the most important gift you'll give your child won't be one of the neatly wrapped packages piled up next to the birthday cake or nestled under the tree, but the memory of celebrations you've shared.

Celebrate Ourselves

Can there be a happier day in a child's year than his or her birthday? Christmas and Chanukah celebrations are wonderful, a Fourth of July party is exciting, a School's Out! party spells fun. But these celebrations belong to everyone -- a birthday celebrates one special person.

Celebrate your child's birthday by working together to plan one of the theme parties in Celebrate! Planning a party is a wonderful opportunity for parents and child to work together and have fun. Together you can select a party theme, make invitations, experiment with different recipes and try new crafts. These parties will take more planning and effort than a send-out-for-pizza-and-rent-a-movie birthday party, but the satisfaction you and your child will experience in working together to make your first piñata or first spaceship cake will more than reward your efforts.

Don't try to do everything in a party plan. We've suggested more for each party than the children will have time to do in two hours. We hope you will alter the party recommendations to suit your needs. If you feel overwhelmed by the idea of preparing lunch, perhaps you should simply bake the special cake and serve punch. Substitute a game or craft from another party if it appeals more to your child than the ideas in the theme party you've selected. The number of ideas you choose from the party plan is not important. What is important is that you and your child are sharing in celebration.

The more you can get done before the party day, the more you will enjoy the celebration. Bake the cake days ahead of time and freeze the unfrosted layers. Thaw and frost the day before the party. Decorate the party room ahead of time and you'll be able to enjoy your decorations longer.

The success of your party depends on the planning. A month before your child's party, sit down together to select a theme. Start with the invitations and list the materials you will need to purchase. Make the invitations and set them aside to send a week before the party. In the weeks before the party, work with your child to make decorations and to shop for party favors. Select crafts and games for the party and purchase the necessary supplies. Look over the suggested menu and recipes and decide what to serve. Shop for food the week of the party.

More hints for successful parties

• Set aside a shelf on which to store materials for party crafts and day-to-day art activities. Keep paste, craft glue and tape on hand. Store pencils, erasers, rulers, markers, crayons and paints in this area, too. Stock colored construc-

Alex, age two

11

- tion paper and newsprint drawing paper, used in many of this book's art activities. Use shoe boxes to collect interesting items, such as gift wrap scraps or ribbon, lace and fabric scraps. Other recyclable items include cardboard inserts from new clothes, foam meat trays, paper towel tubes, broken jewelry, berry baskets, greeting cards, and postcards. Line up the shoe boxes on your shelf and label each with its contents.

- Smaller parties are more fun. A good guideline is to invite the same number of guests as the age of the child. If you feel that is too restrictive, invite 4 to 8 guests for a preschooler's party and 8 to 12 for an older child's party.

- Two hours is ideal for a party that includes lunch. Add half an hour for elementary school children and subtract half an hour for children younger than 4. Remember, the more guests there are, the longer the party should last.

- Jot down a timetable of party activities (guests arrive at 2:00, arrival activity until 2:15, treasure hunt at 2:15, etc.). Add menu items so you don't forget to serve that dish that's hiding behind the milk in the refrigerator. Tape the schedule to a kitchen cabinet for easy reference.

- Always use place markers at the table to eliminate seating disagreements. All parties offer ideas for making place markers, or you can simply write the guests' names on small pieces of folded construction paper.

- If you feel disposable party goods — paper tablecovers, colored plates, napkins and cups — are too expensive, cut costs by using your own tablecloth, dishes and silverware. Decorate inexpensive Styrofoam® cups and napkins with foil stars. Scatter more stars over the tablecloth. Curl 12- to 18-inch lengths of curling ribbon and strew over the table.

- To avoid hurting the feelings of any classmates not invited to the party, don't bring invitations to school. Mail the invitations or deliver them to children's homes.

- Get help in running the party from your spouse, another parent or a babysitter. It's hard for one person to take movies, snap pictures, oversee crafts and serve lunch.

- Set the table ahead of time. If you don't have a second work area, save craft activities until after you've eaten and cleared the table.

- Make sure your house looks like you're having a party. All parties feature decorating ideas, but you can simply tie balloons in front so parents will know where the party is.

- Don't skimp on the quality of balloons. Cheap ones are usually hard to inflate.

- Plan an arrival activity such as working on a simple craft project or decorating favor bags with names and designs. The activity will keep the guests busy until all have arrived. Line up the bags on a table and drop in favors as the party goes on.

- To keep competition to a minimum, don't talk about "winners" and "losers." Give a favor to everyone at the end of each game.

- Alternate quiet crafts and lively games. An activity outside, even in cold weather, helps the children release lots of energy.

- Keep the party out of your child's bedroom. This happens when there's not enough planned activity. Keep the children busy!

- Don't force a child to participate. Some are content to sit and watch.

- Open the presents toward the end of the party. You may want to have something for the guests to do, such as eating juice popsicles or opening their own favors while the birthday child unwraps the presents. "Musical Presents" is a great way to keep the unwrapping orderly. Seat the children in a circle and pass all the presents to music. Whichever present the birthday child is holding when the music stops is the one to open next.

- Have your helper lead songs or read a book to keep the children occupied while waiting for their parents at the end of the party. You'll be busy seeing to the departing guests.

- Take a photograph of each guest at the party as a thank you. Give instant pictures to the children as they leave or mail the photos after they are developed.

Many parents prefer serving a "from-scratch" party cake to using a cake mix. Here is an easy cake that a child can make with a parent's help. You can use it to make the fancy birthday cakes described in the book.

Jessica, age five

13

Happy Party Cake

2 1/4 cups sifted cake flour
1 1/2 cups sugar
2 1/2 teaspoons baking powder
1 teaspoon salt
1/2 cup butter or margarine, softened
1 cup milk
2 eggs
1 teaspoon vanilla extract

1. *Preheat oven to 375 degrees.*
2. *Grease and flour two 9" cake pans.*
3. *Sift together flour, baking powder and salt.*
4. *Cream together butter and sugar in a large bowl, using an electric mixer.*
5. *Add vanilla, then eggs, one at a time. Beat well after each addition.*
6. *Alternately add sifted dry ingredients and milk a third at a time to butter mixture. Begin and end with dry ingredients.*
7. *Pour batter into cake pans. Bake 25-30 minutes.*
8. *Cool in pans for ten minutes. Remove from pans and cool completely on wire racks before frosting.*

Butter Cream Frosting

1/3 cup butter or margarine
1 teaspoon vanilla extract
1/8 teaspoon salt
3 cups unsifted confectioner's sugar
2-3 tablespoons milk

1. *Cream together butter, vanilla and salt.*
2. *Add gradually 1 cup sugar and beat with electric mixer until blended.*
3. *Add 2 tablespoons milk and the remaining sugar and beat until frosting is smooth. Add milk by teaspoons if frosting is too thick.*

Frosts one 9-inch layer cake.

For a frosting with less sugar, try chocolate whipped cream frosting. The cake is best if frosted less than two hours before serving.

Chocolate Whipped Cream Frosting

1/2 cup confectioners' sugar
6 tablespoons unsweetened cocoa
1 pint whipping cream

1. *Sift* together into large bowl sugar and cocoa.
2. *Stir* cream slowly into sugar mixture. Chill at least 2 hours.
3. No more than 2 hours before serving time, *whip* the cream mixture until peaks hold. *Frost* cake and keep in refrigerator until serving.

Frosts one 9-inch layer cake. Refrigerate leftovers.

Mark, age four

Big Top Birthday Party

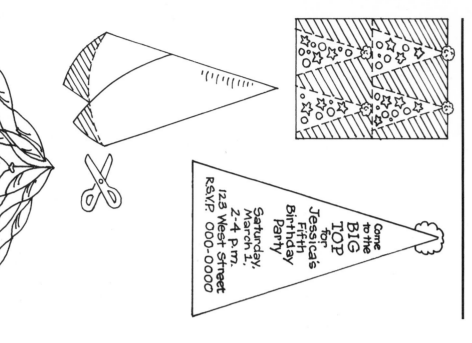

Turn on the circus music! Pipe in some Sousa marches or calliope recordings! Put on your clown hat! Hang streamers and balloons to transform the party room into a lively circus tent for a Big Top Birthday Party! The birthday child would be delighted to have Mom and Dad dress up as clowns for this party, but clown outfits are not necessary. Oversized and wildly-colored clothing, big shoes, and a little makeup will transform you into a wonderful clown.

Clown Hat Invitation

■ 9 x 12" construction paper, adhesive stars, stickers, small pompons, crayons or markers, white craft glue, scissors

1. Cut a triangle from a piece of construction paper. Two triangles cut from one piece of paper make good-sized invitations.
2. Decorate one side with stars, stickers and a pompon on the top.
3. Write the message on the opposite side, using the illustration as a guide.

3-D Clown Hat Invitation
(You'll have to hand deliver this one!)

■ same as above, with the addition of a stapler

1. Form piece of 9 x 12" construction paper into a cone shape.
2. Cut bottom to even off into a clown hat.
3. Unfold and write message on inside.
4. Reform again into a clown hat and staple. The birthday child can decorate the outside with stickers, stars and add a pompon on top. When complete, the hat will be 6" tall.

Decorations

- Hang two or more colors of crepe paper streamers from corners and sides of room to meet in the center like a tent.
- Hang a bunch of balloons in the center. Hang additional balloons around the room.
- Cut multi-colored construction paper triangles, staple to string and hang over the front door.
- Make a sign for the front door that says "Welcome to the Big Top."
- Make circus posters from large pieces of drawing paper or posterboard. You can get good picture ideas from coloring books and children's books. Hang the posters around the room.

Come to the
BIG
TOP
for
Jessica's
Fifth
Birthday
Party

Saturday,
March 1,
2-4 P.m.
123 West Street
R.S.V.P. 000-0000

- Decorate the table with paper cloth and napkins in the bright colors used for the streamers.
- For place cards, write the children's names on bags of popcorn tied with yarn. Circus wagon boxes of animal crackers with the children's names are also a hit as place markers.

Favors

Any circus item such as clown stickers, pens, erasers, small circus animals, animal crackers, balloons, whistles, and paper plate puppets (directions for the puppets are included in the Games and Activities Section.)

Food

Circus Menu
Clown Face Pizzas
Circus Lemonade
Clown Hats and Carousel Cupcakes or
Circus Train Cake

Clown Pizzas
Ingredients: English muffin half for each clown face, pizza sauce, grated cheddar and mozzarella cheese, olive pieces, sausage pieces, and green pepper to make a clown face. *Bake* at 375 degrees until cheese melts.

Circus Lemonade
Decorate a straw with a construction paper clown hat and put it into a glass of pink lemonade. For each clown hat, cut a 2" triangle of construction paper. Punch 2 holes, as in illustration, and put a straw through the holes. Add a few stars or decorate with markers.

Clown Hat and Carousel Cupcakes
For each clown hat you need an ice cream ball, some colorful candy-coated chocolate bits, and a pointed sugar cone. Place an ice cream ball on a plate. Press in the candy bits to make a clown face. Store in the freezer until serving time. When you're ready to serve, top with the ice cream cone "hat." If you wish, decorate the cone ahead of time with frosting, candies, etc. Serve with a carousel cupcake: top a cupcake with a frosted animal cracker prancing under a small paper umbrella.

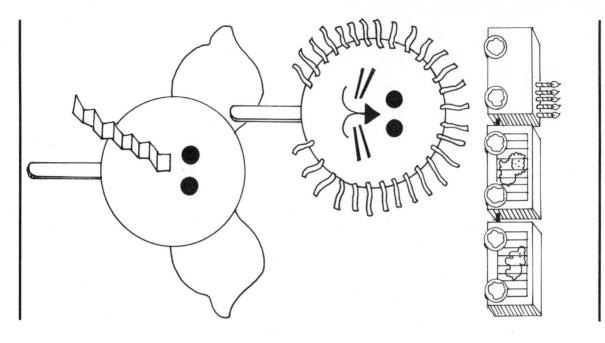

Circus Train Cake

Bake a cake in three small loaf pans or buy three small pound cakes. Frost the "circus cars" and transform them into cages by placing pieces of shoelace licorice over animal crackers on the side of the cakes or by adding bars made of frosting. Add frosted vanilla cookie wheels. Line up "circus cars" and use candles to form the train's engine stack.

Games and Activities

Create a clown's dressing room to transform the party guests into Big Top entertainers as they arrive. A table, mirror and make-up stool under a roof of crepe paper streamers set the atmosphere. Clowns can create their own hats as they wait a turn for make-up.

Clown Face Painting

Decorate the children's faces with acrylic paints or clown make-up. Be sure to take pictures!

Clown Hats

■ 12 x 18" construction paper, scissors, stapler, marker, stickers, stars, pompons, thin elastic or string

Have construction paper cones (clown hats) made up ahead of time. Children decorate their own hats with markers, stickers, stars and pompons. Tie a length of elastic or string through two holes at the base to hold hat on.

Clown Collars

These are fun to do ahead of time with the birthday child.

■ 6 x 24" strips of plastic disposable tablecloth (one for each collar), yarn, large needle, scissors

Sew yarn through one side of plastic strip, gather around child's neck and tie.

Paper Plate Puppets

■ large paper plates, yellow yarn, tongue depressors, pink and black construction paper, craft glue, scissors.

Glue tongue depressors to plates ahead of time. Using the illustrations as a guide, the children can make elephants and lions.
To make masks, cut out holes instead of gluing on eyes.

Parade
Turn up the music and have a parade of the clowns and animal puppets.

Hungry Elephant
Make a funnel ("trunk") from a large piece of paper. Staple elephant ears to the side of the "trunk." Tape to the wall with masking tape or pin by the ears to draperies. Have the children stand ten feet (closer for small children) away from the elephant. They take turns throwing ten peanuts, one at a time, into the trunk.

Lion Tamer
Arrange chairs outward in a circle, using one fewer chair than the number of children. Give each child a picture of a circus animal or performer. Circus coloring books are a good source for pictures. The children all sit down, except for the one child who is the Lion Tamer. The Lion Tamer walks around the circle, calling the names of different circus animals and performers. As the Lion Tamer calls the name of an animal or performer a child has, that child gets up and marches behind the Lion Tamer. When several children are marching, the Lion Tamer calls, "I'm tired. The circus is over" and sits down in one of the vacated chairs. The children rush for the remaining chairs. The child without a seat becomes the new Lion Tamer and the game is played again.

Peanut Relay
Form two teams. Give each team a pile of peanuts, one peanut per team member. One by one, each child must push a peanut with his nose across the room to the finish line.

Circus Tricks
Write the names of circus tricks on pieces of paper. Children pick the tricks out of a clown hat and perform them in pantomime, for all to guess. (Examples: walk a tight rope, tame a lion, perform a flying trapeze stunt.)

Before each performance the other children can chant this First United Nursery School favorite:

"I know a funny clown
His/Her name is Ting-a-ling
He/She does so many funny tricks
When in the circus ring."

Balancing Relay

Divide the children into teams of 3 or 4. Give each team plastic or paper cups and plates. The teams must see how high they can make towers of alternating paper cups and plates before they topple.

Car and Truck Birthday Party

Jessica drives her play car around the patio for hours on end. Mark loves to push his dump truck under the dining room table. Capitalize on your preschooler's favorite pastime and create a Car and Truck Birthday Party. A Car and Truck Party is a wonderful outdoor birthday celebration, but, with a little variation, the children can have as much fun inside.

Traffic Light Invitation

■ black, red, yellow and green 9 x 12" construction paper, scissors, fine black marker or pen, white craft glue

1. *Fold* a 9 x 12" piece of black construction paper in half to make a 9 x 6" card.
2. *Glue* to the front of the invitation, top to bottom, three 2 1/2" construction paper circles - one red, one yellow and one green.
3. *Cut* out a yellow rectangle, 5 1/2 x 8 1/2", and glue to the inside right of the opened invitation.
4. *Cut* out a red stop sign (1 1/2") and a green car (4 x 2") and glue them onto the yellow rectangle of construction paper as in the drawing.
5. *Write* the message, using the illustration as a guide. Add your child's name, party date, etc. For an outdoor party, be sure to tell the guests to bring their own riding vehicles!

Decorations

• Decorate in traffic light colors. Use red, yellow and green streamers and balloons.
• To greet the guests as they arrive, hang a posterboard sign on the garage, fence, or front door, announcing "Mark's Truck Stop," or "Jessica's Service Station."
• Make road signs and traffic signals out of posterboard or construction paper. Hang on trees, fence, garage, etc. Decorate the party room with the signs at an inside party.
• Cover the party table with a disposable white plastic table cover. With permanent marker, draw roads, railroad tracks, and other scenery such as a lake or mountains. Add houses (cover small boxes in white paper and color with markers or crayon), trees (tiny branches stuck in clay), and road signs (glue scraps of construction paper to toothpicks and stick in clay). An older brother or sister might enjoy working on this project with the birthday child.
• For place cards, make stop-sign-shaped signs. Write the guests' names rather than "stop" on the signs. Glue to toothpicks and anchor in clay.

RED

YELLOW

GREEN

STOP whatever you're doing and come to my

CAR & TRUCK

Birthday Party
Saturday, May 30
1 - 2

Mark's house
122 East St.
Bring your vehicle to ride!

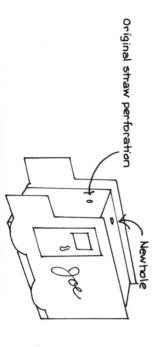

Original straw perforation

Newhole

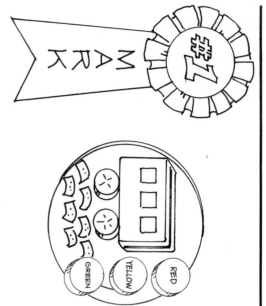

Favors

Car and truck stickers, car coloring books, small metal or plastic cars and trucks, whistles, ribbons for safe driving made from construction paper, marker and adhesive stars or foil notary seals

Food

Trucker's Lunch
Grilled Cheese Buses
Finger Gelatin Traffic Lights
Juice Box Truck (see activities)
Truck Cake or Traffic Sign Cupcakes

Grilled Cheese Buses
Place half a grilled cheese sandwich on a plate. Add carrot disks for wheels and lunch meat squares for windows. Make a bumpy road of corn chips.

Finger Gelatin Traffic Lights
Make three recipes of finger gelatin in traffic signal colors—one lemon, one lime and one cherry, strawberry or raspberry. For each flavor you need:

2 envelopes unflavored gelatin
1 3oz. package flavored gelatin (lemon, lime or cherry)
2 c. boiling water

In a large bowl mix the unflavored gelatin with the flavored gelatin. Add boiling water and stir until gelatin is dissolved. Pour into three 9" square pans. Chill until firm. Cut with small round cookie cutter into traffic lights.

Truck Cake
Cut a square out of the upper right corner of a sheet cake. You will have a very basic truck shape. Frost the cake. With a cake decorating set, write the birthday child's name. Add candy truck lights and chocolate cookies for truck tires.

Traffic Sign Cupcakes
Following the directions under "Decorations," make small traffic signs attached to toothpicks. Stick one in the top of each cupcake and present the cupcakes at the party table in the back of a toy dump truck.

Games And Activities

Juice Box Trucks

■ juice boxes, construction paper, scissors, crayons or markers, white craft glue
For each truck, cut two identical truck shapes a little larger than the long side of the juice box. Have children use markers or crayons to draw windows, doors, and their names, plus other decorations they want. Glue each truck cutout to the long sides of the juice box. An adult can use a knife to make a hole for a straw on the truck's roof (juice box side).

Red Light

The children sit on their vehicles at one end of the driveway or sidewalk. An adult stands at the opposite end of the driveway or sidewalk and calls "green light." At this command, the children ride toward the parent. The parent calls "red light," pauses a few seconds and then turns around. The children must stop immediately when they hear "red light." If the parent sees any child riding, the child must return to the starting point. The game continues until all riders reach the parent. To play inside, have the children line up at one end of a long room holding toy cars. The children push their cars forward on the "green light" command and stop on the "red light" command.

Obstacle Course

Explore the basement and garage with your child to find objects for an obstacle course. Make a tunnel by draping a blanket over two rows of chairs, build a mountain road with a large piece of plywood set on a slight incline. Time the children as they navigate the course. Award safe driving ribbons to all (see Favors). This is fun; allow extra time for the children to ride over the course after their timed runs.

Blocks and Ramps

Set out blocks, long pieces of lightweight wood, oatmeal boxes with two open ends, etc. The children will amaze you with their creativity in designing highways, racetracks and cities. If small cars are given as party favors, now's the time for a test run!

Pass the Truck

Fill a toy dump truck with small favors. Seat children in a circle and let them pass the truck as music plays. When the music is stopped the child holding the truck takes a favor and leaves the circle. Continue the game until all have a favor.

23

Dinosaur Dig Birthday Party

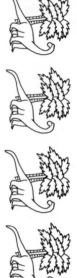

Stegosaurus...Brontosaurus...Tyrannosaurus Rex...If you're excited and intrigued by dinosaurs (and who isn't?), search for fossils in the dining room, gobble a dinosaur for lunch and discover a giant dinosaur egg in your back yard.

Dinosaur Bone Invitation
■ pork or beef rib bones, fine-point indelible marker

1. Scrub rib bones clean and dry in a 200 degree oven for 30 minutes.
2. Write party information in indelible marker on each bone, using the illustration as a guide.
3. Hand deliver the Dinosaur Bone Invitations.

Dinosaur Lover's Invitation
■ 9 x 12" light-colored construction paper, fine- point marker or pen, scissors, dinosaur stickers, envelopes

1. Cut a 9 x 12" piece of construction paper in half to make two 9 x 6" pieces.
2. Fold a 9 x 6" piece in half to form a 4 1/2x6" card.
3. Write the invitation, using the illustration as a guide.
4. Add dinosaur stickers if you wish.
5. Mail or deliver the Dinosaur Lover's Invitation.

Decorations
- Draw a big green dinosaur head on posterboard and hang it on the front door to greet birthday guests as they arrive.
- Decorate the party room with green balloons and streamers.
- Hang posters you've made around the party room.
- Make a dinosaur mural for the party room (see Games and Activities).
- Cover the party table with a green table cover and place mats made by the dinosaur lovers (see Games and Activities).
- Create a dinosaur scene for the center of the table. Put sand in a jelly roll pan or other large pan. Arrange small plastic dinosaurs, small branches, small stones, sprouted carrot tops, mirror-pond, and other items in the sand.
- Use egg-shaped panty hose containers or plastic Easter eggs as place cards. Write the guests' names on the eggs with fine-point indelible marker. As an added surprise, fill the egg with green clay (see Games and Activities).

Come to Jacob's cave for a DINOSAUR DIG Birthday Party on Saturday, Sept. 3 · 12 until 2. R.S.V.P. 000-0000

W•I•L•D* SOCIETY

*We love dinosaurs.

All dinosaur lovers should meet on **Saturday, Sept. 3,** 12 p.m.-2 p.m. at Jacob's house for A Dinosaur Dig Birthday Party

R.S.V.P. 000-0000

Hi, there, Dinosaur lovers!

We love Dinosaurs

DINOSAUR FAN CLUB

Big is BEAUTIFUL!

Favors

Small plastic dinosaurs; plastic eggs filled with green play clay; dinosaur theme items: stickers, pens, pencils, erasers, coloring books, workbooks; egg-shaped malted milk candies; jelly beans

Food

Dinosaur Lover's Lunch
Caveman's Club
Dinosaur Nest
Prehistoric Tree
Breadstick Dinosaur
Iceberg Punch
Dinosaur Dig Cake

Caveman's Club
Serve a chicken leg, hot or cold.

Dinosaur Nest
Grate raw carrots and serve with several pitted black olive dinosaur eggs resting on top.

Prehistoric Tree
Insert a 3 to 4" leafy stalk of celery into a 1 1/2" square, 3/8" thick piece of mozzarella cheese (A slit in the cheese makes it easier to insert the stalk).

Breadstick Dinosaur
■ breadstick dough (eight to a tube, available in the dairy section of the supermarket), raisins

1. *Unroll* a breadstick and cut four pieces about 1/2" long off one end. These will form the dinosaur's feet.
2. *Place* the feet on the sides of the breadstick, leaving one end longer for a tail.
3. *Shape* the tail.
4. *Shape* the head. Slash eye holes with a sharp knife tip and insert quartered raisins for the eyes.
5. *Bake* as directed on the package.

tree

dino eggs

nest

dino

chicken leg

1. Refrigerator breadstick, unrolled

Cut 4 equal pieces for 4 feet

Attach 4 feet on sides

head tapered

Tail curled to one side

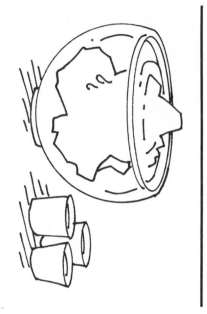

Iceberg Punch

Like a dinosaur, an iceberg is a gigantic, mysterious creation of nature—a fitting addition to a dinosaur lover's lunch. To make an iceberg, fill a plastic bag with about two quarts of water, fasten the top and prop the bag in the freezer until the water freezes. Take the "iceberg" out of the bag and float it in a bowl of punch. Explain to the children that, just as with bigger icebergs, only one-third of their iceberg shows above water...or punch.

Dinosaur Dig Cake

Bake a cake recipe in two 8 or 9" cake pans. Let cool. Spread frosting on the bottom layer. Scatter jelly bean "dinosaur eggs" on the frosted bottom layer so each slice will contain several dinosaur eggs. Add the top layer and finish frosting the cake. Decorate the top of the cake with small plastic dinosaurs. When the cake is served, tell the dinosaur lovers they must hunt for dinosaur eggs in their cake.

Games and Activities

Dinosaur Mural

■ a long length of shelf paper or brown paper, newsprint or drawing paper, markers or crayons, scissors, tape

Before the party, draw a jungle-like scene on a length of paper. Immediately after the children arrive, have them draw various kinds of dinosaurs, color them, and tape them to the mural. The children may create their own prehistoric creatures, or you may use the dinosaur silhouettes pictured at the beginning of this section as models to make dinosaurs for them. Commercially made templates and stencils are also available. After all the dinosaurs are in the jungle, talk about different kinds of dinosaurs or read a dinosaur story.

Dinosaur Place Mats

■ paper place mats or newsprint drawing paper, markers or crayons, clear Con-Tact® paper (optional)

Suggest that the children draw a dinosaur scene or trace their hands and feet to decorate their place mats. If you wish, sandwich each place mat between two pieces of clear Con-Tact® paper. Cut the Con-Tact® paper one inch larger than the place mat to allow for a quarter-inch border.

Play Clay Dinosaur

Make play clay ahead of time and have the children create dinosaurs. Mounting the dinosaurs on a piece of cardboard or a heavy duty paper plate will ensure safe transport home.

Play Clay

Mix together 2 1/4 cups flour, 1 cup salt and 4 tablespoons vegetable oil. Add 1 1/2 cups of boiling water all at once to the mixture. Stir vigorously. When cool, divide into as many small plastic bags as you wish. To make colored play clay, add food coloring to the boiling water.

Fossil Search

Hide scrubbed chicken, rib or other bones around the house or yard. Bones can also be hidden in a sandbox and unearthed with rakes or other tools. If you cannot imagine saving real bones, make cardboard ones. Tell the children to find five bones each and allow them to trade for dinosaur eggs (jelly beans or malted milk eggs).

Dinosaur Bone Relay

Two teams stand in lines. Give a "dinosaur bone," real or cardboard, to the first child in each line. In turn, team members must do the "dinosaur walk" (walking on all fours and roaring) to a goal, return, and hand the bone to the next team member.

Dinosaur Hunt
(Recommended for older children)

Place small plastic dinosaurs in obvious places around the house or yard. Tell the children they have one minute to walk around noting the dinosaurs' locations. They should not talk. After the minute is up, take the children to a different spot where they must make a list of the places they saw the dinosaurs, i.e., "yellow dinosaur on top of the TV" or "green dinosaur under the blue chair."

Volcano

Were erupting volcanoes one of the reasons for the disappearance of the dinosaurs? No one knows. You can experience your own erupting volcano at your party. Before the party, line a suit box lid with foil and fill it with wet sand. Place an empty soup can in the center of the box and press the sand around the can to form a mountain, completely concealing the can. Put 1/4 cup baking soda in the can and place the box on a surface protected with a plastic drop cloth or newspapers. When it is time for the volcano to erupt pour a portion of the following solution into the hidden can: mix together 1 cup water, 3/4 cup vinegar, 1/2 cup dishwashing liquid, 10 drops of red food coloring and 10 drops of yellow food coloring. When the solution is added to the baking soda, the lava will flow. The party guests can take turns adding a bit of solution to the can to cause further eruptions.

juice can

"lava"

sand

Box lined with foil

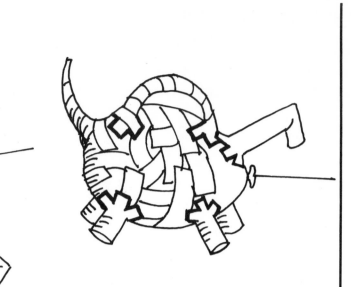

Dinosaur Piñata

■ a large balloon, papier-mâché (newspaper strips or paper towel pieces soaked in a flour and water mixture), paper towel rolls, poster paint, brushes

1. *Blow up and tie a large balloon.*

2. *Tie a sturdy string to the balloon and suspend the balloon from a basement beam, ceiling hook, tree branch or other stable support. Be sure to cover the floor underneath with a drop cloth or newspapers.*

3. *Mix one part flour and two parts water to a cream-like consistency.*

4. *Dip paper towels or newspaper strips into the paste and cover the surface of the balloon with the papier-mâché. Two or three layers of papier-mâché make a sufficiently sturdy piñata for small children. Five or six layers are needed for older children. The balloon will "stretch out" of the papier-mâché covering at the point it's hanging. Don't worry about covering this area. The uncovered area will allow a space to pop the balloon when the papier-mâché is dry and provide an opening to fill the piñata with the candy and favors.*

5. *Make a handle on the piñata by twisting a paper towel or piece of newspaper into a rope. Drench it in paste and lay the ends on the balloon, securing with papier-mâché. (See illustration.) This handle will allow the piñata to be hung for the game.*

6. *Bend one end of a paper towel roll to form a dinosaur head. Make four or five 1-inch slices on the other end of the roll. Splay the cut end onto the body of the dinosaur and secure with papier-mâché. Add legs in a similar fashion with shorter piece of paper towel roll. Cover the neck, head and legs with one layer of papier-mâché. A few pieces of papier-mâché will form a tail. Let is dry completely.*

7. *Paint the piñata green or mottled green and brown or cover with pieces of crushed green crepe paper. Let dry.*

8. *Pop the balloon, fill the piñata with party favors, peanuts, gum, wrapped candy and other goodies. Cover the opening with a couple layers of masking tape or a layer of papier-mâché. Paint.*

9. *Hang the piñata from a tree branch or ceiling hook. One by one the blindfolded children take turns swinging a stick to break open the piñata. Note: By following these basic piñata instructions, you can make any sort of animal by changing features and color. You may also choose simply to decorate the balloon shape by gluing on colorful crumpled crepe paper, tissue paper shapes, or crepe paper streamers.*

Dinosaur Egg Hunt

For the most adventure, play this game outside. Tell the children there is a dinosaur egg—it's big and it's green—hidden somewhere in the yard. The children hunt until someone finds the dinosaur egg - a watermelon. Everyone wins a refreshing cold slice.

An Enchanted Birthday Party

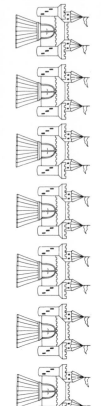

Abracadabra! A wave of your magic wand turns a party room into a wonderland of giant flowers and colorful balloons. Touch the heads of your guests with your wand, and they become princesses and princes in golden and glittered crowns. Let the enchantment begin!

Magic Wand Invitation

■ 9 x 12" construction paper, unbendable plastic straws, marker or crayon, adhesive foil stars, scissors, #10 envelopes and optional glitter writer

1. Cut out two stars about 3" wide and 4" long.
2. *Write* the invitation on the stars, following the illustration.
3. *Glue* the end of a straw sandwiched between the two stars.
4. *Decorate* the invitation with glitter writer and adhesive foil stars if desired.
5. *Hand deliver* the Magic Wand Invitations or *mail* in large envelopes.

Decorations

• Create an enchanting party room. Choose a lively color scheme, such as pink and orange, green and pink, or purple and red. Use your two colors for crepe paper streamers, balloons, a table covering, plates, napkins and cups.
• Make large paper flowers to hang on the walls.

Paper Flowers

■ sheets of paper or tissue paper to match your color scheme, scissors, glue, stapler

1. Cut out three scalloped flower shapes (each a different color), the largest about 12 inches across, the second about 10 inches and the third about 8 inches.
2. *Stack* the three flowers, largest on bottom, smallest on top.
3. *Staple* or *glue* them together in the center.
4. *Glue* a contrasting 3" circle to the center.
5. *Hang* on the wall with a loop of masking tape on the back of the flower.

- Add a balloon bouquet. On the day of the party, buy a bunch of helium balloons. Tie the balloon strings together at the ends and anchor them in a large flower pot. Stuff green tissue paper leaves into the pot. Tie green ribbon curls to the ends of the balloons. Set the bouquet outside the front door to welcome your guests. After everyone arrives, bring it inside as a floor decoration.
- For a table centerpiece, follow the directions for making crowns in Games and Activities section. Create a crown with sequins, glitter marker, etc. Place a bowl of flowers inside the crown (use real flowers or make crepe paper flowers, directions page 81).
- Make crown name cards. Cut a small paper crown two inches high from construction paper. Write guest's name with marker or glitter writer on the crown. Glue around a paper nut cup filled with raisins.

Favors

Masks; crowns or scarf hats (directions under Games and Activities); play jewelry; star, unicorn or dragon stickers; fancy pencils

Food

Enchanted Luncheon

Main Course
Unicorn Punch
Princess Cake

Main Course

An elegant lunch of fancy little delectables will certainly enchant the visiting princesses and princes. Pick some of these or add your own ideas:

Fancy sandwiches: cut bread with cookie cutters and spread with cream cheese or peanut butter; decorate with your choice of walnuts, sliced strawberries, raisins, grapes, sunflower seeds, olives, etc.

Tiny sandwiches of cream cheese on date nut, pumpkin or cranberry bread

Ham and cheese sandwiches on party rye or whole wheat, cut into party shapes

Peanut butter sandwiches with paper-thin apple slices on white bread

Applewiches: peanut butter spread between two apple slices

Stuffed cucumber: Peel cucumber, cut off one end. Scoop seeds out with an infant-feeding spoon or blunt knife. Stuff hollowed-out cucumber with cream cheese. Slice cucumber into 1/2" circles.

Skewered fruit pieces

Raw vegetables and dip

Carrot curls

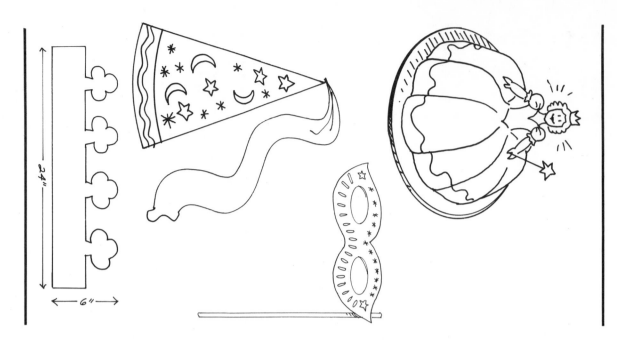

24"

6"

Unicorn Punch

One 40-oz. bottle apple juice, chilled

Two 12-oz. cans apricot nectar, chilled

One 6-oz. can frozen lemonade concentrate, thawed

One 1-liter bottle lemon-lime soda or orange soda

Stir these ingredients together and pour into glasses. You may add a scoop of orange sherbet and a cherry to each glass. Decorate the glass with a few adhesive foil stars.

Princess Cake

Bake a bundt cake. At a craft store, purchase an inexpensive doll about 8" tall. Stand the doll in the hole of the cake. Using a pastel frosting, ice the cake to look like a princess's dress. Add sprinkles, silver decorations, candy pieces, etc. Put icing on the doll's bodice to complete the dress.

Games and Activities

Have the children make masks and crowns or scarf hats as soon as they arrive to give them princess and prince props.

Masks

■ heavy white posterboard or white cardboard, scissors, marker, glitter writer, feathers, craft glue, thin dowels 18" long, craft knife

Before the party, cut out the masks. Use a craft knife to cut out the eye holes. Glue on the dowel rod and allow to dry. At the party, the children decorate the masks with marker, glitter, feathers, and sequins.

Crowns

■ craft glue, stapler, light-weight gold or yellow posterboard, craft feathers, sequins, pompons, lace remnants, and bits of ribbon

Cut out the crowns before the party. Using the diagram as a guide, make one crown for each child from a 6 x 24" piece of posterboard. Use the first crown cut as a template for the remainder of the crowns. At the party the children decorate the crowns with the feathers, lace, and sequins. Let the glue dry and staple the crowns to fit each child.

Scarf Hats

■ cone-shaped party hats, pieces of chiffon-like fabric (about 3 x 18"), stars, lace, and sequins

Children staple scarf to the hat's point and add adhesive stars, sequins, etc. Some children may wish to eliminate the scarves and concentrate on the other materials.

Croak, Toad, Croak

The children squat, toad-style, in a circle. A blindfolded person designated as It squats in the center of the circle and holds a wooden spoon. It squat-walks towards the other children, who are the toads, with the spoon extended. When the bowl of the spoon touches a toad, It says, "Croak, toad, croak." It must guess the identity of the toad. It may ask the toad to croak three times. The toad becomes the next It.

Who Has Gone?

It is blindfolded and told that an evil sorcerer has made one of the children disappear, and It has the power to bring the child back. It stands in the center of a circle of seated children. One child from the circle quietly leaves the room. The children sing this verse to the tune "Jingle Bells:"

Who has gone,
Who has gone,
Who has gone away?
Now's the time for you to say
Who has gone away. Hey!

At the end of the song, It takes off the blindfold and must quickly look around and guess who has disappeared. The child who left the room becomes the next It.

Dress-Up Relay

Divide the children into two teams. Give each team a bag with a similar selection of clothing and accessories: wig, hat, dress, gloves, shoes, jewelry, etc. At the signal, the first member of each team puts on all the items in the bag, picks up the bag, runs to a designated spot, takes off all the relay clothing, puts the items back into the bag, runs back to the team, and gives the bag to the next member. The game ends when all members dress, undress, and run back to the start.

Enchanted Waltz

Give each child a scarf or left-over length of chiffon. Have them wear their hats or crowns. Play waltz or other dance music and invite the children to move to the music in your "grand ballroom."

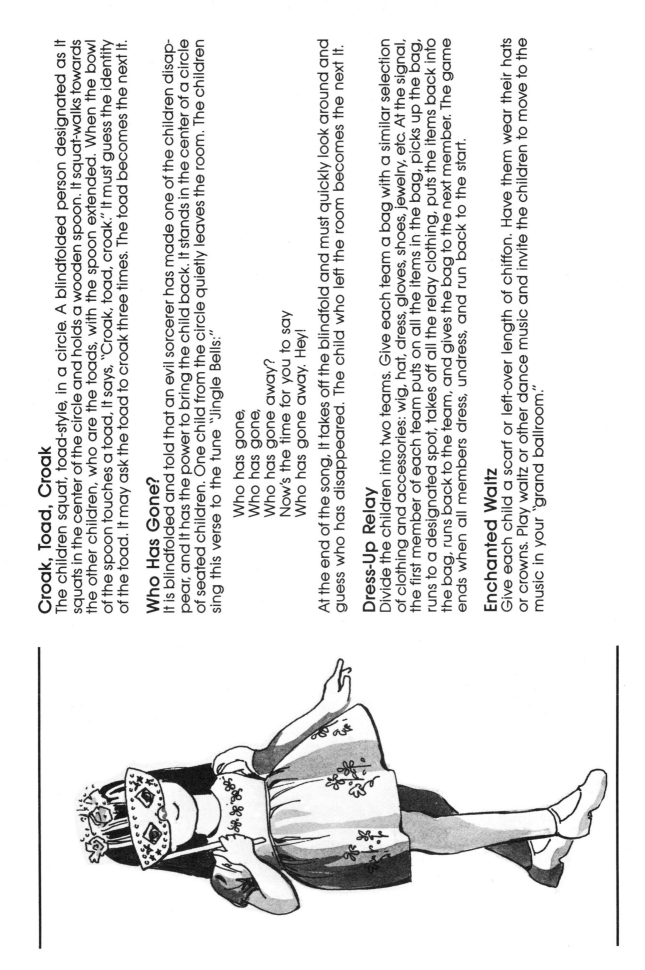

Fun in the Sun Birthday Party

If you're lucky enough to celebrate a birthday during the summer months, party under the sun. Put on your sunglasses and head to your back yard, a nearby park or the beach for active games and sunshiny food.

Happy Sun Invitation

■ yellow and orange construction paper; scissors; paste or glue; marker, pen or crayons; envelopes

1. Cut out an orange sun shape about 3 1/2" across to fit into an envelope. (Illustration 1)
2. Cut out a yellow disk about 2" across.
3. Glue the yellow disk onto the orange sun.
4. Draw a happy sun face with red crayon or marker. (Illustration 2)
5. Write the invitation on the reverse side. (Illustration 3)
6. Mail or deliver the Happy Sun Invitations.

Decorations

- Make a big "Sunshine Hello" from yellow posterboard and hang the greeting on a fence, tree, gate or garage.
- Attach a bunch of helium-filled yellow, orange and red balloons to the fence, porch railing, etc.
- Tie more yellow, orange and red balloons (not helium-filled) to tree branches to make a Balloon Tree.
- Hang yellow, red and orange streamers from the tree branches; drape more streamers over the fence and shrubs.
- Cover the picnic table in a sunshine-yellow tablecloth or eat picnic style in the grass.
- Put pinwheels into a bucket of sand for a lively table centerpiece.
- Use bottles of bubbles for place cards. Remove the labels and write each child's name with indelible marker.

Favors

Plastic bottles of bubbles, large sidewalk chalk, sunglasses, plastic sand buckets, Frisbees®, pinwheels, small rubber balls, and salt scenes and sun visors (See Games and Activities).

It's time for "Fun in the Sun." Saturday, May 30 12-2 at Mark's Wear your swim suit!

1.

2.

3.

Hello!

KIM

Food

Younger Children's Menu
Pack each lunch in a sand bucket.
Happy Face Sandwiches
Fresh Fruit
Giant Sunshine Cookies
Juice Boxes or Pouches

Happy Face Sandwiches
Spread peanut butter on rice cakes. Add raisin faces. Wrap loosely in plastic wrap.

Giant Sunshine Cookies
Cut out giant cookies from your favorite sugar cookie recipe. Bake and cool. Pipe on happy faces.

Older Children's Menu
Serve on new inverted Frisbees®. If you're traveling to the park or beach, pack each lunch with its Frisbee® in a large paper bag. Freezing the juice boxes or pouches will keep each lunch cool.

Pocket Chicken Sandwiches
Skewered Fresh Fruits
Chips
Sunshine Cake
Juice Boxes or Pouches

Pocket Chicken Sandwiches
Fill pita bread with diced cooked chicken. Offer a variety of sandwich toppings: grated cheddar cheese, chopped tomatoes, shredded lettuce, sprouts, olives, etc.

Sunshine Cake
Bake an 8 or 9" layer cake. Let cool. Frost with white icing. Pipe on a smiling yellow sunshine face.

Games and Activities

Paper Plate Sun Visors
■ paper plates (not foam or cardboard), markers or crayons, scissors, hole punch, paper ring reinforcers, 1/4" elastic
1. *Cut a paper plate, discarding the smaller portion.*
2. *Decorate the visor with crayons or markers.*

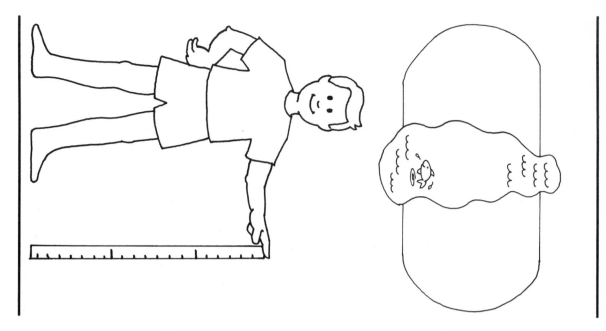

3. With a hole punch, *punch* one hole on each side of the visor and attach reinforcers.

4. *Thread* a length of elastic through the holes, adjusting to fit the child's head. Tie.

Colored Salt Scenes

■ baby food jars, salt, colored chalk, white craft glue

1. *Pour* salt into small bowls, one bowl for each color.
2. *Rub* the sticks of chalk back and forth through the salt to color it.
3. *Layer* the colored salt to the top of the jar. The designs will resemble the desert, the ocean and southwestern rock formations.
4. *Squirt* a layer of white craft glue over the salt.
5. *Apply* glue to the inside threads of the jar lid and screw on the lid.

Handle carefully so as not to disturb the design.

Variation: Instead of replacing the salt layers with glue, sprinkle colored aquarium sand onto the wet glue. Handle carefully.

Doodle Trip

Give each child a piece of paper and a pencil or a crayon. Have the children make one squiggly line, all over the paper. They have just made a map for a "doodle trip." The children must follow the route of their maps around the yard. They can also trade maps to take each other's trips.

Crossing Rainbow Lake

Draw a large broken oval, about 3 feet by 10 feet on the driveway, patio, or sidewalk. Draw a lake across the broken section of the oval. The lake must be large enough so the children cannot jump or step over it. Play music while the children walk around the oval. When the music stops, any children in Rainbow Lake must remain in the lake for the rest of the game. The game continues until all the children are in the lake.

Catch It If You Can

(recommended for older children)

All the players stand in a circle to create a human sundial and are given a number. The child who is It stands inside the circle and holds a yardstick with just one finger on the top of the yardstick; the other end of the yardstick stands on the ground. To play, It lifts a finger, allowing the yardstick to fall, and at the same time calls a number. The player with that number must catch the yardstick before it touches the ground. If the yardstick touches the ground before the child whose number was called catches it, he or she becomes It. If the child whose number was called succeeds in catching the yardstick, It must call another number.

Wet Buckets

Line up five buckets, one behind the other. Fill with water. The children form a line about three feet from the first bucket. Give each child in turn five rubber balls, one to throw in each bucket.

Pass the Sand Relay

The children sit in the grass in two rows. At the front of each row, place a bucket of sand and at the rear, an empty bucket. Give each child a spoon. The first child in each row takes a spoonful of sand from the bucket and must pour the sand into the spoon of the next child, who then passes the sand to the next child and so on down the row. The last child in each row pours the sand into the bucket at the end of the row. The children continue passing sand until the buckets are emptied.

Wading Pool Guess

Have the children take turns sitting blindfolded in a wading pool with 2-inches of water. Float five or six items in the water; an empty foam egg carton, a sponge, a plastic spoon, or a baby bottle are suggestions. Each child must find and identify as many items as possible in a minute. Try to use different items for each child. Note: A parent must carefully monitor this game.

Sun Prints

Purchase photo-sensitive paper at a hobby store or specialty toy store. The children arrange leaves, feathers, lace bits, etc., on the paper and expose the paper to the sun. After washing in water, a sun print appears. Fascinating for children of all ages.

If it rains, don't despair! Have fun in the sun inside under a big posterboard sun. Decorate the party room with all your sunshiny balloons and streamers. Most of the games can be played inside with slight variations. For "Crossing Rainbow Lake," use chalk on the basement floor or masking tape to mark the broken oval and lake. Play "Wet Buckets" with dry buckets. Use an empty wading pool for the "Wading Pool Guess." Have your lunch picnic style, on the floor under your indoor sun.

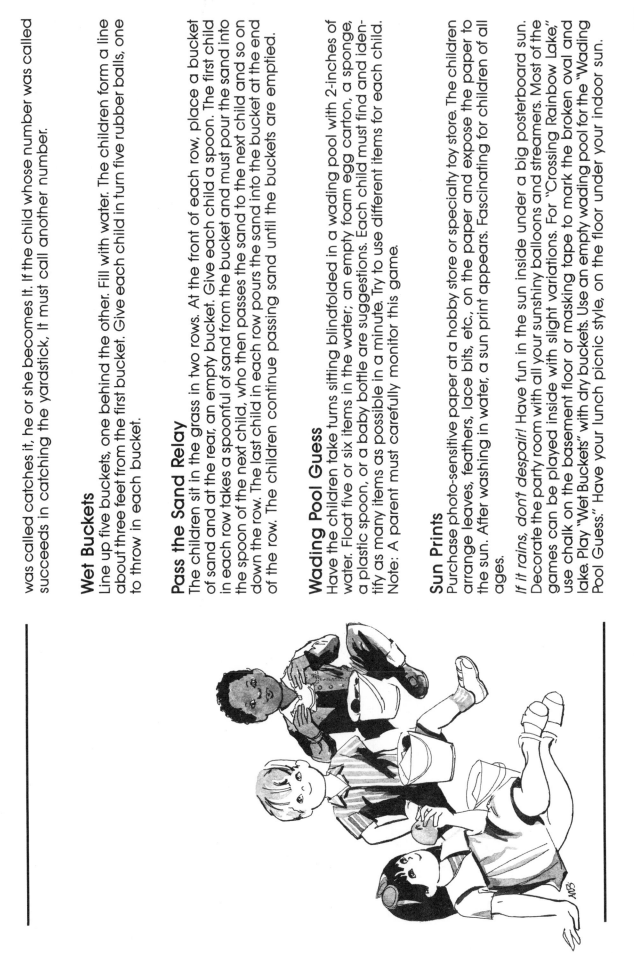

Jolly Roger Birthday Party

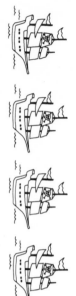

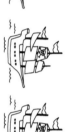

Avast me hearties! If setting sail under the Jolly Roger flag sounds exciting, invite your friends to come aboard your pirate ship. Be careful when you walk the plank— there are alligators below! With your mates safely on board, cast off to hunt for pirate treasure. Ahoy!

AHOY, MATES!
Sail with Jacobs'
Band of Birthday Pirates
on Sunday, September 15
from 2 until 4

N
W   E
S

SEEK
BURIED
TREASURE!
X

RAINBOW LAKE

SHIP OF SURPRISES

Captain Jacobs' Treasure

Treasure Map Invitation

■ envelopes, large brown bags, markers, scissors, ribbon, yarn or string

1. Cut out an irregularly-shaped treasure map, about 10 x 12", from a brown bag.
2. Write the invitation using the illustration as a guide.
3. Singe the edges of the map to make it look very old. Make sure an adult does this step.
4. Roll up the map, tie with ribbon, yarn or string, and hand deliver, or fold the invitation to fit the envelope and mail.

Decorations

- Make a Jolly Roger Flag (2 x 3') from an old sheet or fabric remnant. Draw a skull and crossbones with black indelible marker. Tie two corners onto a stick and hang the flag near the front door.
- Make treasure-map place mats from large brown bags (see Games and Activities). These can be used later to find a buried treasure.
- Use red, black and white balloons, streamers, table cover, plates, cups and napkins to decorate the room.
- Cut out gold coins from construction paper and sprinkle them over the table.
- For a centerpiece, fill a treasure chest with Gold Doubloon Cupcakes (see Food). To make the treasure chest, use gold spray paint to cover the outside of a large shoe box. With indelible black marker, draw on a lock, skull and crossbones. Add the words "Captain Jacobs' Treasure."

Favors

Pirate hats and eye patches (see Games and Activities), bandanas, tatoo decals, toy telescopes and periscopes, foil-wrapped chocolate coins, small plastic boats

Food

Pirate Galley Lunch

Fleet of Pirate Ships
Fish-shaped Crackers
Fruit on a Sword

Pieces of Eight
Pirate Punch
Gold Doubloon Cupcakes

Fleet of Pirate Ships

Fill three-inch pieces of celery with peanut butter, cream cheese or cheese spread. Run toothpicks through one-inch paper sails and insert into the celery filling. Add raisin "pirates."

Fruit on a Sword

Purchase sword-shaped plastic picks. Spear several chunks of fruit onto each pick.

Pieces of Eight

Serve slices of raw carrot, zucchini, and cucumbers, but call them "Pieces of Eight" rather than "vegetables."

Pirate Punch

Mix one part lemon-lime soda and two parts of grape juice.

Gold Doubloon Cupcakes

Top frosted cupcakes with foil-wrapped chocolate coins. Hide the cupcakes in the treasure chest centerpiece. Add a candle to the birthday child's cupcake.

Games and Activities

Deck out the mates in pirate garb as they arrive:

- Use a burnt cork or charcoal to give the children beards.
- Buy black eye patches or make them out of black construction paper glued to 1/4" elastic.
- "Tatoo" the children with tatoo decals or acrylic paint.
- Let each child make a telescope from paper towel rolls and decorate with crayon or marker.
- Tie on red bandanas, pirate style. If you wish, ahead of time, sew a gold-colored curtain ring to each bandana for an earring. Tie a bandana on your child to determine where to place the earring.

Pirate Hats

■ lightweight white posterboard, scissors, markers, stapler

1. *Cut out* two hat shapes, about 5 x14", for each pirate hat. Use the illustration as a guide.
2. *Have* the children decorate their hats with their names and drawings of anchors, pirate ships, treasure, or skull and crossbones.
3. *Staple* the two parts of the hat together at points a and b to fit the child.

Treasure Chest Game

Put a treasure (gold-coin candy, gum or pirate stickers) into a cash box that locks with a key or into a box to which you have attached a padlock with a keyhole. Line up the children and give the key that will open the lock along with several others to the first child. The child must decide which key will open the Treasure Chest. The child keeps trying different keys until the Chest opens and he or she selects a treasure. The chest is locked again. The game continues until all the children have opened the Treasure Chest and claimed their treasure.

Captain Hook Relay

Make cardboard hooks, one for each child. The children stand in two rows and hold their hooks. Place a bangle bracelet or rubber canning ring over the first child's hook. The children pass the ring from hook to hook.

Treasure Hunt

(The lunch place mat also serves as the treasure map for this game.) Pairs of children will search for several treasures in this game. Draw a map, 10 x 12", of your yard or house. Singe the edges of the map. Put prizes into containers and hide them around the yard or house. For example, you might hide a container of wrapped gum sticks, a container of balloons, and a container of toy telescopes. Mark an X on the map to show the locations of the hidden treasures. Give each child a small bag to hold the prizes. The children follow their maps in search of the treasures and take one item from each container.

Jolly Roger Treasure Map

Walk the Plank

Use masking tape to make a pirates' gang plank, 3 x 8', on the floor. One at a time, blindfold the children, spin them around three times, and ask them to walk from one end of the gangplank to the other without falling to the alligators.

Magic Magnet Birthday Party

What an attraction! Your friends will be irresistibly drawn to your party when they hear about the magnet games you've planned. You won't have to force them to eat magnet sandwiches or magnet birthday cake either!

Magnet Invitation

■ silver posterboard, red indelible marker, black fine-point marker, scissors, large envelopes

1. *Cut* out a horseshoe-magnet shape, 5 x 6", from the posterboard.
2. *Highlight* the front with red marker to make it resemble a magnet.
3. *Write* the invitation in black marker on the reverse side of the magnet.

Note: as an alternative, use red posterboard and highlight with black marker.

Decorations

• Hang on the front door a stenciled sign proclaiming "Jessica's Science Lab."
• Make more stenciled signs such as you'd see in a laboratory and hang them around the party room, for example, "No Smoking," "Danger-Chemicals," "Do Not Enter Lab - Employees Only," "All Employees Must Wear ID Tags," or "Experiment in Progress."
• Decorate in magnet colors, silver and red. Cover the table with a disposable silver cover. Use clear cups with ounces marked in indelible pen to resemble laboratory beakers. Add red plates and napkins.
• Hang several small horseshoe magnets with attracted metal items such as safety pins, paper clips, nails or tacks over the center of the table.
• Hang red and silver balloons and streamers.
• Write the children's names in indelible marker on real horseshoe magnets and use them as place cards.

Favors

ID Badges (See Games and Activities), compasses, magnets, guests' names spelled out in magnetic letters, small magnet games

Food

Magnificent Magnet Lunch
Magnet Sandwiches
Crunchy Apple Banana Salad
Do-It-Yourself Lab Sodas
Magnet Cake

cut away shaded areas

Magnet Sandwiches

2 1/4-ounce can deviled ham
1/2 cup grated Swiss cheese
1 teaspoon prepared mustard
1 package 10 refrigerated biscuits
(poppy seeds or sesame seeds, optional)

Heat the oven to 350 degrees. Grease a muffin pan. Combine the first three ingredients in a bowl. Separate the biscuits and roll them into ten 4-inch circles. Spread one tablespoon of the ham and cheese mixture onto each of the circles. Roll up with the filling inside and curve into a U-shape. Place one U-shaped roll with the ends up into each muffin cup. Brush with milk and sprinkle ends with seeds. Bake at 350 degrees, 15-20 minutes or until golden. Makes ten.

Do-It-Yourself Lab Soda

10-ounce clear plastic cups with ounces marked in indelible ink, straws, tablespoons

Provide a selection of beverages, ginger ale, lemon-lime soda, and root beer, along with ice cream and whipped cream. Give the children instructions to follow so they can concoct their sodas scientifically. For example, you might say, "Put ice cream in your glass up to the 3-ounce mark, add 5 ounces of a liquid, then drop in 1 tablespoon of whipped cream." Serve with straws and spoons.

Crunchy Apple-Banana Salad

3 medium apples, 2 bananas, 1 celery stalk, 1 cup sour cream or plain yogurt, 1/4 cup frozen orange juice concentrate, thawed

Wash the apples and cut them into bite-sized pieces. Peel and slice the bananas. Chop the celery into small pieces. Combine and toss with sour cream or plain yogurt and frozen orange juice concentrate. Serves 8.

Magnet Cake

Bake a 9 x 13" cake. Let cool and cut into a horseshoe magnet shape as illustrated. Frost in white and sprinkle red sugar on magnet's ends.

Games and Activities

ID Badges

■ 3 x 5" index cards, red marker, black fine-tip marker, instant camera and film, glue, masking tape, safety pins, scissors

Complete steps 1-3 before the party.

1. *Outline* the edges of an index card in red marker.
2. *Write* "Jessica's Science Lab" (use your child's name) and the party guest's name on the badge.
3. *Tape* a safety pin to the back of the badge.
4. *Take* an instant photo of each child. If no instant camera is available, ask each child to bring a photo to the party.
5. *Cut* the photo to fit the upper left of the ID Badge and glue on.
6. *Pin* the badge to the child's "lab coat." Since it might take some time for all children to receive their ID Badges, you may want to plan an activity such as coloring favor bags for some children to work on as others get their IDs.

Magnet Experiments

With their magnet place cards, children can experiment with magnetic force. On a table place many items, some that will be attracted to the magnets and some that will not - paper clips, coins, aluminum foil, silver-colored plastic buttons, spoons, nails, nuts, bolts and wood. You'll also need a shallow dish of water and a few pieces of paper and fabric. Ask the children to consider questions such as:

1. Which materials are attracted to your magnet?
2. Which materials are not attracted to your magnet?
3. What is the strongest part of your magnet?
4. Through which materials will your magnet work?
5. What happens if you try to put two magnets together?
6. Will your magnet attract objects if they are under water?
7. How can you make magnets out of paper clips?

Making a Compass

Unbelievable as it seems, a compass points to the north because the magnetic needle is attracted to huge ore deposits under the North Pole. You can make your own compass and watch it spin around to point to the North Pole.

■ steel sewing needles, corks (available at hardware stores and hobby shops), small nails

1. *Magnetize* a needle by rubbing it thirty times in one direction on a magnet. Test to see if the needle is magnetized and rub longer if necessary.
2. *Insert* a nail vertically about 1/4" into the bottom of the cork.
3. *Insert* the needle horizontally through the opposite end of the cork.
4. *Place* the cork in a container of water and the needle will point to the North Pole.

JESSICA'S
SCIENCE
LAB

LILY   # 3 2 1 3 0

Magnetic Car Race

■ 22 x 28" lightweight posterboard, car stickers or 2" construction-paper car cutouts, markers, paper clips, scissors

1. Cut each piece of posterboard into four 11 x 14" pieces. Give one piece to each of the children.
2. Have the children *draw* racetracks on their posterboard.
3. *Sandwich* a paper clip between two car stickers or attach a paper clip to a construction-paper car. Give one car to each child.
4. Have the children put their cars on the tracks and move their magnets under the posterboard to race the cars around the tracks.

Magnet Fishing

Attach paper clips to light objects: wrapped sticks of gum, small pieces of wrapped candy, play rings, stickers, and other favors. Put the items into a large bowl. Make a fishing pole with a dowel and a magnet "hook" tied to a string. The children take turns fishing for prizes.

Magnet Alphabet Bingo

Cut construction paper into two-inch squares. Print a letter and fasten a paper clip to each square. Make bingo cards from construction paper, using the same letters. Children take turns fishing the letters out of a container with a magnetic fishing pole (see Magnet Fishing). As each letter is called, the children cross it off their bingo cards. Variation: Place one paper clip on each square of the bingo card. As a letter is called, the children use small straight magnets to remove the paper clip from the square called.

Robot Power Cell

Draw a large robot on shelf paper and hang it on the refrigerator. The children take turns being blindfolded and trying to put a magnet as close to the robot's power cell as possible.

Rodeo Roundup Birthday Party

Round up your cowpoke friends for a rootin' tootin' good birthday time. Play recordings of cowboy favorites such as "O Susanna" and "Get Along Little Dogie" or Aaron Copland's "Rodeo" or "Billy the Kid." Put on your ten-gallon hat, tie on your bandana and get ready for chuckwagon grub and rodeo games.

Lasso Invitation

■ cotton clothesline, string, construction paper, hole punch, paper reinforcers, fine-point marker or pen

1. *Tie* a 12" length of rope into a lasso.
2. *Write* the invitation on a 3 x 5" piece of construction paper, using the illustration as a guide.
3. *Punch* a hole in the invitation and put a paper reinforcer around the hole.
4. *Tie* the invitation onto the lasso with a piece of string.
5. *Hand deliver* the Lasso Invitation.

Wanted Poster Invitation

■ typing paper, fine-point black marker, envelopes

1. *Print* and *draw* the invitation using the illustration as a guide.
2. *Photocopy* as many copies as you need.
3. *Mail* the Wanted Poster Invitations.

Decorations

- Make a rustic sign from cardboard for the front door.
- Draw cattle brands on large pieces of newsprint and hang them around the party room.
- Illustrate other western themes by drawing cowboy hats, cactuses, horses, campfires and saddles on newsprint. Have the birthday child color the pictures or invite arriving guests to decorate and hang the drawings.
- For a centerpiece, build a small pretend campfire from sticks. Cut flames out of cardboard or posterboard and color the front and back with markers or crayons to resemble a fire. Prop the cardboard flames between the logs or tack the flames to the sticks.
- Spread a red checkered tablecloth on the table. Use bandanas for napkins. Serve the lunch in metal pie pans and the beverage in mugs.

Howdy, Pardner!
Mosey on over to Cowboy Mark's Ranch on Saturday, November 3, from 12 to 2, for a Rodeo Roundup Birthday Party. Chuckwagon grub served and rodeo games played! All cowpokes should wear western duds!

YOU ARE
WANTED
for
MARK'S RODEO ROUNDUP BIRTHDAY PARTY
Saturday, November 3
12 - 2
Chuckwagon Grub and Rodeo Games

Wear your western duds!

WELCOME TO
MARK'S RODEO

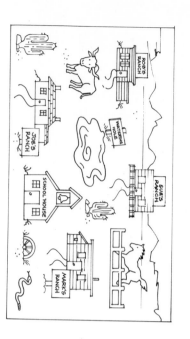

Food

Chuckwagon Grub Lunch

Cowpoke Beans and Franks
Diamond Branding Irons
Texas Toast

Beef Jerky
Ten-Gallon Punch
Corral Cake

Cowpoke Beans and Franks

Slice hot dogs into a saucepan of canned baked beans. Heat and serve in metal pie pans.

Diamond Branding Irons

Cut 3/4" thick mozzarella or muenster cheese into 1" long diamond shapes. Slit a 1/4" deep small cross in the top of the cheese. Insert a thin 3" long carrot stick into the cheese to make a branding iron.

Texas Toast

Toast slices of bread, spread with butter, and cut into 3 strips. Serve toast strips in a bandana-lined basket.

Beef Jerky

Purchase beef jerky and let the children sample a food similar to that eaten by cowboys of the Old West.

Ten Gallon Punch

Mix equal parts of lemon-lime soda and cranberry juice. Serve in mugs.

Corral Cake

Bake a 9 x 13" cake. Let cool and frost with caramel or light chocolate icing. Make a corral fence by standing thin pretzel stick halves in a crisscross fashion around the top of the cake. Put a few small plastic cowboys and horses in the corral. Put the candles in the center of the corral, lean-to style. When lit, the candles will look like a campfire.

Favors

Sheriff badges, red bandanas, bags of gum nuggets, drawstring bags of foil-covered chocolate coins, western stickers, and branding iron stamps and horse puppets (see Games and Activities)

Games and Activities

Branding Iron Stamps

■ unsharpened pencils, thin cardboard, white craft glue, scissors, inked stamp pad, paper

1. *Cut out* a one-inch square piece of cardboard.
2. *Glue* the cardboard square to the top of the pencil eraser. (Illustration 1)
3. *Allow* to dry overnight.
4. *Give* each child a one-inch cardboard square on which to draw a simple branding iron design. Be sure the design is VERY simple as it must be cut out. (Illustration 2)
5. *Cut out* the brand.
6. *Glue* the brand *in reverse* to the cardboard previously glued to the pencil. (Illustration 3)
7. *Allow* to *dry* for thirty minutes.
8. *Press* the branding iron stamp onto a stamp pad and have the children brand large cutout paper cattle.

Horse Puppet

■ brown construction paper, black marker or crayon, red yarn, tape, hole punch, scissors

1. *Fold* a 9 x 12" piece of construction paper in half to make a 6 x 9" foldover.
2. *Draw* a horse's head using the illustration as a guide.
3. *Cut out* the horse's head through the two thicknesses of paper. The cut out should be as close to 6 x 9" as possible.
4. *Punch* holes about an inch apart, 1/4" from the edge.
5. *Wrap* 2" of tape around the end of an 18" length of yarn. The taped yarn end forms a needle to make it easier for children to lace the yarn through the holes.
6. *Tie* the untaped yarn end to the first hole in the puppet.
7. *Have* the children lace the horse puppets. Knot the ends of the yarn when the children finish sewing.
8. *Encourage* the children to add eyes, mouths, manes, and bridles. When all the puppets are completed, play western music and parade the horse puppets around your corral.

cut away shaded area

1

2

3

cutting line

Wild Horse Roundup

The children sit in a circle. One child is the cowboy and asks one of the group, "Have you seen my horse? She's wearing a red sweater and blue skirt." The child asked looks around the circle, spots the cowboy's "horse" and chases her around the outside of the circle. If he catches the horse she becomes the cowboy. If he doesn't catch her, he becomes the cowboy.

Branded Cow

It, the branded cow, chases the other children, the unbranded cows. Whichever unbranded cows It touches also become branded cows and must hold the body part tagged with one of their hands. The newly branded cows join It in trying to tag the other unbranded cows. The last unbranded cow becomes It for a new game.

Where's the Ranch

Draw a map of a western town. Decorate with western symbols and include all the party guests' "ranches." One by one, give the children western stickers, blindfold them and turn them around three times. They walk toward the map and see how close to the birthday child's "ranch" they can get their stickers. Each child has a turn.

Cowpoke Course

In this obstacle course, children execute a series of cowhand tasks. Give the first child a cowbell, or any bell, which must be carried throughout the entire course. First, the child runs to a bucket of water, ladle and cup. The guest uses the ladle to fill the cup. He or she then runs with the filled cup and the bell to a stick horse (make one out of an old stuffed sock, tied to a wooden yardstick). The child pours the water into the horse's drinking trough, a bucket or bowl. Mounting the horse, and still carrying the bell, the child rides to the woodpile, a pile of twigs or cardboard logs. The cowhand dismounts, picks up three twigs, and runs with the bell to a pretend campfire. The nearly exhausted guest then puts the three twigs on the fire and unrolls a waiting sleeping bag or rolled-up blanket. He or she puts the bell down and pretends to go to sleep in the sleeping bag. An adult returns all the items to their original spots and gives the bell to the next child. After all the cowpokes have completed their tasks, they gather at the campfire to sing some songs or read a story about the Wild West.

Space Voyage Birthday

The word "astronaut" comes from the Greek words for "star" and "ship." Invite your friends to join the crew of your starship for a birthday voyage to outer space. Blast off to birthday fun!

3-D Rocket Invitation

■ blue and white construction paper, red or orange curled ribbon, white craft glue, stapler, blue and red marker or crayon, scissors

1. Cut out a white construction paper rectangle, 5 x 7".
2. Write the invitation in red and blue marker or crayon, using Illustration 1 as a guide. Leave a 1" margin along the 7" sides.
3. Roll the rectangle into a 5" long cylinder. Be sure not to cover up any of the message.
4. Staple the edges.
5. Cut out a 4 1/2" blue construction paper circle. This is the nose cone.
6. Cut from the circle's outer edge to the center, as in Illustration 2, and roll into a double-thick cone. Staple to hold.
7. Cut five 18" lengths of red or orange ribbon. Tie the ribbons together at one end and loosely curl the ribbon. Tape to the inside tip of the nose cone.
8. Glue the nose cone to the top of the rocket body. The curled ribbon will run through the rocket's body and emerge at the other end.
9. Decorate the rocket with adhesive foil stars.
10. Hand deliver the Rocket Invitation.

Silver Star Ship Invitation

■ light weight silver posterboard, adhesive foil stars, indelible black marker, scissors, #10 business envelopes

1. Cut out a space ship, about 3 x 7".
2. Write the party information, using the illustration as a guide.
3. Decorate the invitation with colored foil stars.
4. Mail the Silver Star Ship Invitation.

49

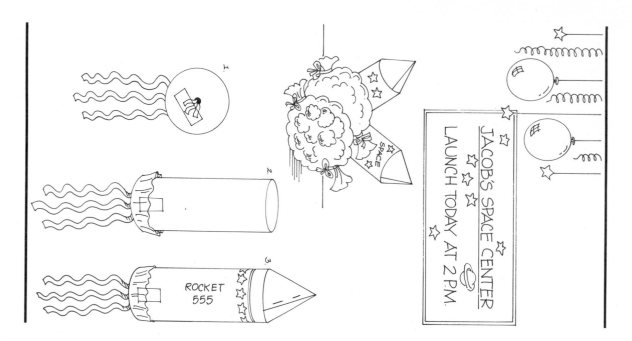

Decorations

- Make a blue posterboard sign decorated with silver adhesive stars and silver glitter writer to hang on the front door.
- Create an illusion of space by hanging a Milky Way of silver posterboard stars. The Milky Way is a band of many faint stars that make a dim milky glow in the sky.
- Suspend silver and blue balloons on silver ribbon from the ceiling. Tape strands of silver Christmas tree icicles to the balloons for extra dazzle.
- Hang long lengths of curled silver ribbon among the balloons.
- Use a dark blue disposable table cover, red plates and cups.
- Make star-shaped placemats from silver posterboard or large pieces of foil-covered cardboard. Use red glitter marker or red indelible marker to write the crew's names on their placemats.
- Arrange asteroid and rocket favors on the table as the centerpiece.

Asteroids

Wrap a handful of popcorn in clear wrap. Twist the ends and tie with curled silver ribbon.

Favor-Filled Rockets

■ toilet tissue tubes, red and white construction paper, red or orange curling ribbon, scissors, white craft glue, stapler and tape

1. Cut out a 4" white construction paper circle.
2. Poke a hole in the center of the circle and insert three 8" lengths of red or orange ribbon, loosely curled. Tape to hold the ribbon in place (Illustration 1).
3. Cover one end of the tube with the construction paper circle. Be sure the ribbons hang outside the tube (Illustration 2).
4. Crimp the paper circle up and around the bottom of the tube and tape in place.
5. Cover the entire tube with white construction paper and glue in place.
6. Roll a nose cone of red construction paper and staple.
7. Fill the rocket with small party favors (see Favors).
8. Glue the nose cone to the top of the rocket.
9. Decorate as desired.

Favors

Rockets (see Decorations) filled with small plastic figures attached to parachutes, rocket erasers, space stickers, and silver-wrapped chocolate kisses; popcorn asteroids (see Decorations).

Food

Star Ship Lunch
Orbiting Orange
Celery Rocket
Flying Saucer Toast
Foil-pouch Drink
Space Ship Cake

Orbiting Orange
1. *Place* an orange half, cut side down, on a plate.
2. *Spear* an assortment of foods — cheese cubes, chunks of cucumber, morsels of cooked chicken, carrot curls—on toothpicks and insert into the orange.

Celery Rocket
1. *Cut* wide pieces of celery into 6-inch lengths.
2. *Cut* one end of each celery piece into a point.
3. *Cross cut* one inch of the reverse end and soak in cold water for several hours until the celery pieces curl.
4. *Fill* with cream cheese and add olive slice portholes.

Flying Saucer Toast
1. *Cut* bread into circles with a 3-4" cutter.
2. *Spread* with butter or margarine and sprinkle the top with parmesan cheese.
3. *Place* under the broiler for 2-3 minutes until the cheese is bubbly and golden brown.

Space Ship Cake
1. *Bake* a 9" layer cake. Cool.
2. *Cut* each layer as in Illustration 1.
3. *Arrange* the pieces into a two-layer cake as in Illustration 2.
4. *Use* white frosting between the layers and to attach the smaller pieces to the main section.
5. *Finish frosting* the cake with white icing and add silver cake decorating balls, black shoestring licorice, and red LifeSavers®.
6. *Serve* the Space Ship Cake on foil-covered heavy cardboard or a baking sheet with stars scattered about.

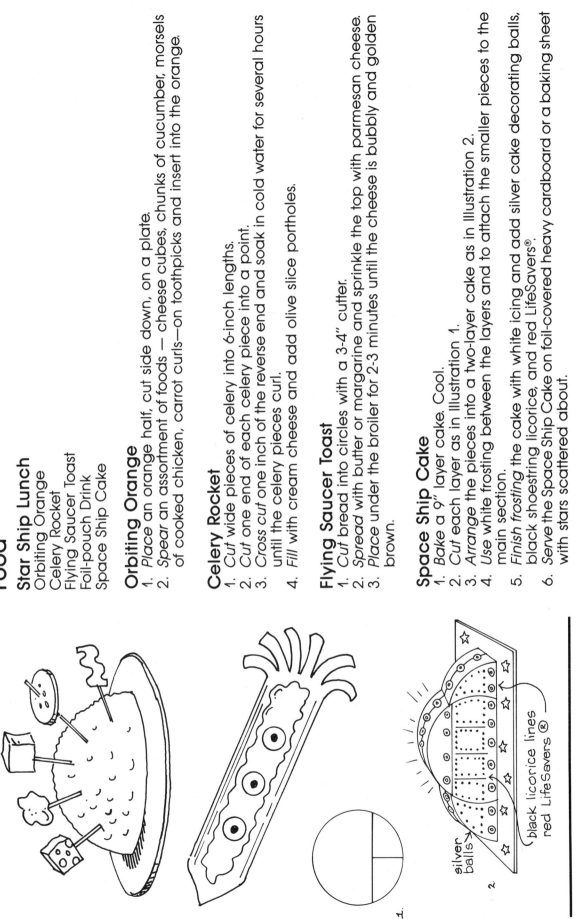

silver balls
black licorice lines
red LifeSavers ®

1.

2.

Games and Activities

Space Helmets

As the children arrive, they can make space helmets to wear for the party. Below are two plans for very individual helmet creations. Complete steps 1 and 2 before the party.

■ plastic gallon milk containers or three-gallon ice cream containers,silver spray paint, scissors or craft knife, indelible markers, adhesive foil stars, sequins, pipe cleaners, nails, bolts, nuts, paper clips, white craft glue

1. Cut the milk container, as in Illustration 1, or the ice cream container, as in Illustration 2.
2. Spray the container silver.
3. Spread a variety of the decorating items listed above in the center of a cloth.
4. Give each child a container to decorate.
5. Allow some time for the helmets to dry. A hairdryer will speed the process.

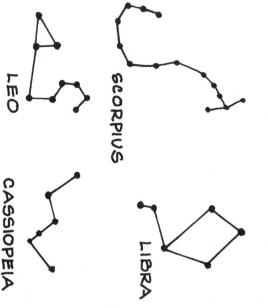

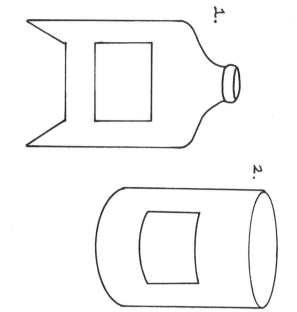

SCORPIUS

LIBRA

LEO

CASSIOPEIA

Astronaut Food Activity

Quarters are tight on board a space ship, so astronauts eat compact food similar to the freeze-dried food sold in stores which feature camping and backpacking equipment. Grocery stores also stock freeze-dried items such as dried soup in plastic cups. Purchase several freeze-dried items for a tasting session. Most foods are prepared by adding water (boiling or cold, depending on the food) to the foil container or plastic cup.

Constellation Viewing

In ancient times, people looked up to the sky and imagined that groups of stars looked like animals, people or things. They called these star groups "constellations," Latin for "together starred." The ancient people found 88 constellations, gave them names, and told wonderful stories about the star groups. Make a constellation projector from a soup can or an oatmeal box. An adult should help punch holes in the bottom of the can or box with a nail. Use the illustrations of constellations below as a guide. Shine a flashlight through the opened end of the can and project the stars onto the wall or ceiling. The constellation will show up more clearly in a partially darkened room or under a blanket-covered table. Before the party prepare several cans and label them with constellation names. The space crew will enjoy projecting the images themselves.

Constellation Hopscotch

Tape paper stars to the floor in the shape of a constellation. The children hop on one foot from one star to another around the constellation. If the party is outside, draw the constellation on the sidewalk with chalk.

Moon Rocks

Astronauts wear special equipment for working in space. For this game the children should wear space helmets and astronaut gloves (a pair of mens large work gloves). Mark a spot to be the moon and a spot to be the space station. The space crew stands at the space station. Scatter many moon rocks (crumpled balls of foil) on the moon. The first child puts on the gloves, picks up a small bucket and runs to the moon. On the moon, the astronaut loads three rocks into the bucket, carries the bucket back to the space station, dumps the moon rocks out, and passes the gloves and bucket to the next player who repeats the process. For a more competitive game, divide into two crews and see which crew collects all of their moon rocks first.

Space Walk

For younger children make a large circle of different color construction paper stars taped to the floor. Have as many stars as children at the party. For older children cut out paper circles and on each write the name of a planet. Write the colors of the stars or the names of the planets on small pieces of paper and put them into a bowl. As music is played, the children step from star to star or planet to planet. When the music stops, each child freezes on his or her star or planet. An adult draws a paper from the bowl. The child on the star or planet drawn receives a star sticker on his hand or helmet. Continue playing until everyone earns a star or two.

5-4-3-2-1 Blast Off!

Everyone is It in this game of tag. Players tag each other; a tagged player is frozen. The game begins with an adult shouting "5-4-3-2-1 Blast Off!" The player left in motion after all others are frozen gives the countdown which puts everyone back in motion to play again.

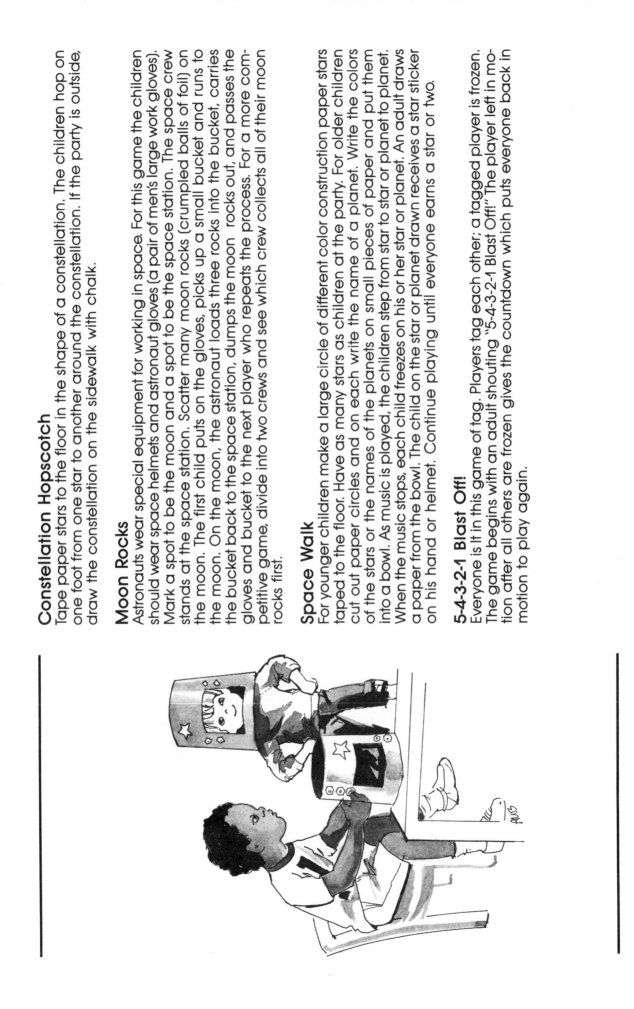

Sports Tourney Birthday Party

Do your children and their friends like to play soccer and baseball? Celebrate a birthday by inviting friends to take part in a tourney of sports games and relay races. Highlight your party with an awards banquet after the games.

Sports Invitation

■ pages torn from sports magazines (pick colorful, action photos or illustrations), construction paper, fine-point marker or pen, tape or glue, scissors, envelopes.

1. Cut out an award ribbon (4 x 8") from construction paper (Illustration 1).
2. Write the invitation on the ribbon, using Illustration 2 as a guide.
3. Tape or glue the award ribbon to the magazine page as in Illustration 3.
4. Fold and mail.

Play Ball Invitation

■ play baseballs and fine-point indelible marker

Use the illustration as a guide to word your party invitation. Hand deliver.

Decorations

- Select a color scheme—your favorite team's colors, perhaps—for streamers, balloons and table cover.
- Decorate with large drawings of sports items: pennants, baseballs, soccer balls, footballs, basketballs, goal posts. Cut out the drawings and hang them around the party room.
- Make trophy place cards. Cover small pudding boxes, or boxes of similar size, with aluminum foil. Cover four-inch cardboard circles with aluminum foil. Decorate the circles with adhesive foil stars and write the guests' names in indelible marker or red glitter marker. Make a one-inch slit on the front side of the box and insert the circle.
- Make a larger version of the trophy place card for a centerpiece. Follow the directions above using a shoe box and an eight-inch cardboard circle. Decorate both sides of the circle with adhesive stars. Write "All-Star Sports Banquet" in indelible marker or red glitter marker.

Favors

Keychains with footballs, baseballs or pennants; sports stickers; sports trading cards; pencils, pens or notepads with team logos; iron-on patches; foil-wrapped chocolate footballs; pennants (see Games and Activities)

Many towns have all-sports stores which sell both national and local team items. You can find many items for party favors, such as pens, pennants or patches with team logos. Look for local team items in variety and department stores. College gift shops and high school pep clubs offer items ranging from buttons to notebooks.

Food

All-Star Sports Banquet

Fifty Yard Line Sandwich
Play Ball Salad
Shoestring Potatoes

Playing Field Cake
Cranberry Cooler

Fifty Yard Line Sandwich

Make a giant submarine sandwich for the sports fans!

Ingredients: French or Italian bread in long, thin unsliced loaves
Lunch meat and cheeses, select a few: salami, baloney, ham, roast beef, chicken, provolone, Swiss or American cheese
Shredded lettuce
Sliced tomatoes
Optional: olive oil, vinegar, sliced pickles, oregano

Slice loaves in half lengthwise but don't cut all the way through the loaves. Open the loaf and pull out some of the bread from one side to form an indentation to hold the sandwich contents. Lay slices of meat on the bottom half of the loaf. Top with a layer of cheese slices. Add additional layers of meat and cheese if desired. Add shredded lettuce and sliced tomatoes. If you wish, add pickle slices and sprinkle with a little vinegar, olive oil and oregano. Close the Fifty Yard Line Sandwich. Cut two-inch pennants from construction paper and mark with yardage or team names. Run toothpicks through the pennants. Slice sandwich into three-inch portions and insert a pennant into each piece.

Play Ball Salad

Use a melon baller to scoop out watermelon, cantaloupe and honeydew balls. Add ball-shaped fruits such as grapes and blueberries.

Playing Field Cake

Bake a 9 x 13" cake. Let cool. Frost with a pale green icing. Pipe on boundaries and yardage lines with chocolate icing. To make a goal post, slit two straws near the top and insert a third straw into the slits. Place the goal post at one end of the cake. Repeat for the second goal post. Add sports figures to the field.

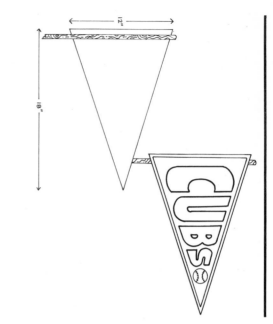

image**★★★ Official! ★★★**
THROW, KICK and PASS
Certificate

This certificate declares

Jane Smith

threw a baseball __25__ feet

kicked a soccerball __50__ feet

passed a football __20__ feet

Date: *June 4, 1986*

#1

Cranberry Cooler

For two quarts mix together:

1 quart cranberry juice
1 cup grapefruit juice
1 cup orange juice

Chill the above ingredients. At serving time, add 2 cups of ginger ale. Serve in paper cups decorated with adhesive foil stars and sports stickers.

Games and Activities

Pennants

Make the pennants as the first party activity. That way, the glue will dry during the games.

■ colored lightweight posterboard, scissors, markers, construction paper, white craft glue, and thin dowel rods, 24" long

If you decide to make local team pennants, purchase colored posterboard and construction paper in team colors. Otherwise, provide a selection of colors for the children to design their own.

1. Cut out a pennant, 12 x 18 ", from posterboard.
2. Cut out letters and team symbols from construction paper.
3. Highlight with markers.
4. Glue a dowel rod on the back of the pennant and let dry at least 30 minutes.
5. Wave your pennant!

Sports Tourney Games

Your back yard is a good spot for the sports tourney games. If you live near a park or playground with playground equipment and a ball field, you'll have more room. Carry along a cooler of cold water and paper cups to provide thirst-quenchers between events.

Group Calisthenics

Lead the group in a round of jumping jacks, squat thrusts and sit-ups to get all warmed up for the sports games to follow.

Throw, Kick and Pass

You'll need a very long tape measure for this game. To make a sports tape measure, mark a ten-yard length of heavy string into feet with indelible marker. Wrap red tape at the yard marks and indicate the yardage. Wind the measure onto a stick to keep it from getting tangled. For the game, lay the sports tape measure along the area where the children will throw, kick and pass. Each child has three turns to throw a baseball, kick a soccer ball and pass a football. Jot down the distances and record the best distances for each event on certificates you've made ahead of time. Present each child with a "Throw, Kick and Pass Certificate" at the All-Star Sports Banquet.

Time Out

The children stand in a circle facing the center. They put both hands behind their backs. All but one child is given a sports item such as a baseball, catcher's mitt, soccer ball, or ice skate. The children pass the items behind their backs around the circle. When an adult calls, "Time Out," the children stop passing the items. Whoever is not holding something goes to the center of the circle. Take away one item for each child who leaves the circle. The game continues until only one child holds an item. More than one child may be without an item in a round because other children could be holding two items when "Time Out" is called.

All-Sports Obstacle Course

Make an obstacle course of five sports feats. Set up the course in the back yard or at the park, incorporating the playground equipment into the obstacle course. Mark each obstacle with a red flag or other marker. Children like to be timed on obstacle courses; be sure to have a stop watch or watch with a second hand. The following is an example of a sports obstacle course. The child runs from "start" to a basketball, picks up the ball and shoots a basket. The next step might be to dribble the basketball a distance to a soccer ball. The contestant must kick the soccer ball to a goal. He or she then runs to the playground chinning bar and completes five chin-ups. Record the children's times on construction paper sports ribbons you've made ahead of time. Present the ribbons at the banquet.

Around the Bases

Mark home plate, first, second and third bases in your back yard or use the neighborhood ball diamond for this game. The first child picks up a baseball bat, tosses a ball into the air and hits the ball. He runs to first base. He must then do forward rolls from first base to second base. He hops on one foot from second base to third base and does a crab walk from third base to home plate. You can time this game and write the times on award ribbons to present at the banquet.

Awards Banquet

Begin the banquet by singing "Take Me Out to the Ballgame." During the meal play tapes of college fight songs and other sports music such as "The Super Bowl Shuffle." After the meal, present the certificates and ribbons individually with great fanfare.

Mix together an assortment of good friends costumed as "Stars," a party room decorated in silver and the fun of dramatic play. Add a Superstar Supper and a Star-Studded Breakfast. Sprinkle generously with surprises and you have the recipe for a Star Sleepover Birthday Party.

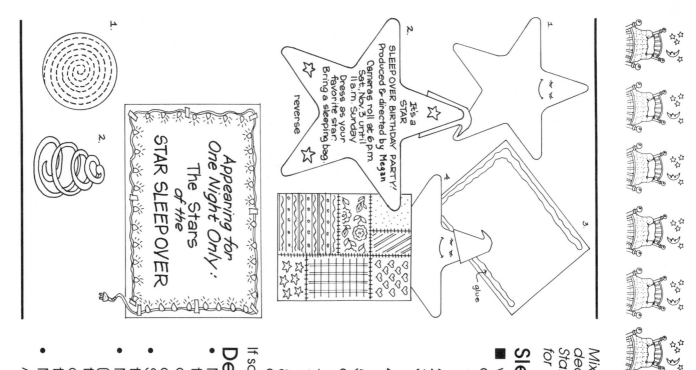

Sleepy Star Invitation

■ white and colored construction paper, scissors, fine-point black marker, glue, crayons or markers, #10 envelopes

1. Cut out a star, 4 x 4", from white construction paper. (A 4" cookie cutter makes a good template.)
2. Draw a face on the star with a fine-point black marker, as in Illustration 1.
3. Cut out a 1" nightcap from colored construction paper and glue it to the top of the star.
4. Write the party message on the reverse side of the star using Illustration 2 as a guide.
5. Cut out two colored construction paper rectangles, 3 1/2 x 4".
6. Apply glue to the edges of the 4" sides and one of the 3 1/2" sides of one of the rectangles. Do not apply glue to the remaining 3 1/2" side.
7. Place the second rectangle on top of the glued side of the first rectangle to form a "sleeping bag." Be sure one 3 1/2" side opens.
8. Decorate the sleeping bag with crayons or markers in a patchwork pattern.
9. Slip the star into the sleeping bag so it peeks out, as in Illustration 3.

If some children are unable to spend the night, invite them for dinner and games.

Decorations

- Make a glittering sign for the front door: Tape a string of Christmas lights around the edge of a 2 x 3' piece of heavy posterboard. Plug into an extension cord and turn on the sign to greet the arriving "stars." Move the sign to the party room after everyone arrives.
- Suspend various sized silver and pink posterboard stars from the ceiling. Write the names of the party guests on some of the stars.
- Make fancy spirals to hang from the ceiling. Cut circles of varying diameters (6", 8", 10") from pink construction paper. Make one continuous spiralling cut from the outside of the circle to the center, as in Illustration 1. Pick up the small center section of the circle and the cut circle will fall into a spiral, see Illustration 2. Tape the spirals to the ceiling.
- Make a "Star Walk," a sidewalk for the Stars to autograph. (See Games and Activities.)

- Decorate the party table in pink and silver. Cover the table with a disposable silver table cover. Set the places with white doily placemats, pink plates, cups and napkins. Decorate the cups with several foil adhesive stars. Scatter pink ribbon curls around the table.

- Hang a cluster of pink balloons over the table. *Blow up 9-11 balloons. Tie long pieces of curling ribbon to each balloon. Use loops of masking tape to stick the balloons to each other. Hang the balloon cluster from the ceiling with an uncurled piece of ribbon. Curl the remaining ribbons. Decorate the balloons with foil adhesive stars.*

Star Place cards and Centerpieces
1. *Cut out two identical stars, 4 x 4", from pink or silver posterboard.*
2. *Write the guest's name on both stars.*
3. *Glue the stars together with a 6" wooden pick glued between them. Let dry.*
4. *Cover a piece of Styrofoam®, 1 x 2 x 3", with foil. Insert the wooden pick.*

- Use the star motif for the centerpiece, too:
1. *Make five to seven additional star picks of various heights.*
2. *Write phrases describing the birthday child's star qualities on both sides.*
3. *Cover a piece of 1" Styrofoam®, about 6 x 8" with foil. Insert the star picks.*

Favors
Fancy Sunglasses (see Games and Activities), play jewelry, small plastic picture frames, combs, buttons, stickers, autograph books, fancy pencils

Food
Children always seem to be hungry — especially at a sleepover! Here are menus and recipes to supply nourishment for the stars at dinner and breakfast.

Super Star Supper
Tinseltown Tacos
Salad Roll
Raspberry Punch
Brownie Star Sundaes

Tinseltown Tacos
Make taco filling according to your favorite recipe. Fill the taco shells with the mixture and invite the children to add their choice of condiments: grated cheddar cheese, chopped tomatoes, shredded lettuce, sliced black olives, chopped green onions, and sour cream or plain yogurt.

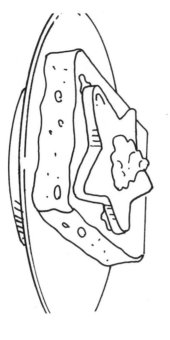
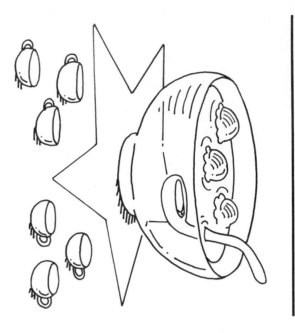

Salad Roll

For each salad roll: 1 lettuce leaf, cream cheese, 1 thin carrot stick, 1 thin celery stick, 1 thin cucumber stick. Spread each lettuce leaf with a thin layer of softened cream cheese. Put the vegetable sticks at one end of the lettuce and roll up the lettuce leaf. Secure with a frilled toothpick.

Raspberry Punch

Place scoops of raspberry sherbet (1 quart) into a punch bowl. Add one liter of chilled lemon-lime soda. Makes about 10 6-ounce servings.

Brownie Star Sundaes

Ingredients: brownies, one 3" square for each child; 1/2 gallon vanilla ice cream in a block carton; chocolate syrup; chopped nuts; whipped cream; cherries and other toppings

1. *Cover* a baking sheet with foil and place it in the freezer.
2. Be sure the ice cream is very firm. You must work quickly. *Cut away the card-board ice cream container and remove the half-gallon block.*
3. With a long thin knife, *cut a 1" slice of ice cream from the narrow end of the block.* *Return remaining ice cream to freezer.*
4. *Use a 3 - 4" star-shaped cookie cutter to cut out two or three ice cream stars.*
5. With a spatula, *slide the ice cream stars onto the baking sheet in the freezer.*
6. *Cut another 1" slice and continue cutting out stars until you have enough.* *Sprinkle* with colored sugar or other decorative topping.
7. When the ice cream stars are firm, *cover* the baking sheet with plastic wrap and store in the freezer until serving time. If you plan to store the ice cream longer than 24 hours, wrap each star individually in foil.
8. At serving time, *place* one brownie on each plate. *Top* with an ice cream star.
9. *Allow* the children to select and add their own toppings.

Star-Studded Breakfast

Star French Toast
Ham-It-Up Roll
Blushing OJ

Star French Toast

Ingredients: 8 slices bread, 4 eggs, 1 cup milk, 1 tsp vanilla extract, 1/4 tsp cinnamon, butter or margarine, syrup

1. *Cut* slices of bread into stars with a 4" cookie cutter. Save the bread scraps to make bread pudding or stuffing.

2. *Beat* together the eggs, milk, vanilla extract and cinnamon.
3. *Melt* 1 tablespoon butter or margarine in a large skillet.
4. *Dip* bread stars into the egg mixture; place in hot skillet.
5. *Cook* over medium heat until one side is lightly browned. Turn and brown the other side.
6. *Add* more butter to the pan to cook additional bread stars.
7. *Serve* with syrup. Makes eight 4" French toast stars.

Ham-It-Up Roll
Ingredients: thin slices of baked or boiled ham, pineapple chunks, frilled toothpicks

1. *Roll up* a slice of ham.
2. *Spear* a pineapple chunk with a frilled toothpick and insert into ham roll.

Blushing OJ
Puree eight to ten very ripe strawberries in a blender or mash by hand in a bowl. Mix into 48 ounces of orange juice. Garnish each glass with a strawberry if you wish.

Games and Activities

Star Sidewalk
Tape a long piece of white butcher paper or brown wrapping paper to the floor. Glue on cut-out stars with the guests' names. As the children arrive, have them autograph the paper near their names and trace their hands and feet to leave "prints." They can use their own names for autographing or use names of celebrities whose identity they assume for the night.

Fancy Sunglasses
■ inexpensive children's sunglasses, craft feathers, sequins, ribbons, lace, white craft glue, scissors

1. *Cover* a table with newspaper.
2. *Spread* the decorating items on the table.
3. *Give* each child a pair of sunglasses to adorn with feathers, sequins, ribbon and lace.
4. *Be sure* to photograph the stars in their glasses.

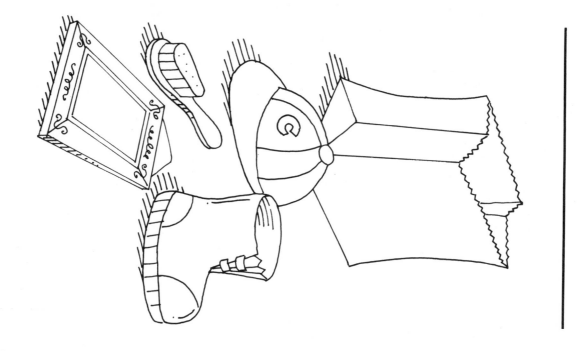

Life-Sized Stars

Position each child on his or her back on a long piece of paper (butcher paper or brown wrapping paper). Draw an outline of each child and have the children transform the outlines into self-portraits with crayons, markers or poster paint. Hang the creations around the party room.

Famous Name Guess

Write the names of famous people — entertainers, sports personalities and historical figures — on index cards. Tape one index card to each child's back. Be sure the children don't know which names they have. At a signal, all the children ask each other questions that will reveal the identity of their famous names. The game continues until all the children have guessed their famous names.

Bag Plays

Divide the children into two or three groups. Give each group a grocery bag filled with a different assortment of items. For example, a bag could be filled with a can of soup, an old boot, a picture frame, a hairbrush, and a newspaper. Each group has ten minutes to put together a short play using all the items in the bag without adding other props. Each group presents their play to the others. If you have video equipment, be sure to tape the dramatics and have a "world premiere."

Funny Fortunes

Before the party, compose enough funny fortunes so each child will have a few. Personalize the fortunes to mention favorite entertainers and interests. Sample fortunes are: "You will star in a movie," "a famous artist wants to paint your portrait," or "the President has declared your birthday a national holiday." Write the fortunes on small slips of paper and put into a bowl. At the party have the children take turns drawing the fortunes and reading them out loud.

Memory Test

Here's a challenge to sharpen the stars' memories. Seat the children in a circle and tell them to carefully observe one child who slowly turns in the center of the circle. That child then leaves the room and changes one thing about his or her appearance. The child might switch a watch from left to right wrist, take off a belt, roll up a sleeve or untie a shoelace. The child returns to the center of the circle and the other children must guess what has been changed. The first child to guess correctly becomes the next child in the center of the circle.

Hollywood

The children sit in a circle. An adult announces a number, 5 for example. One by one the children count around and around the circle. Whenever a number which contains a 5 or is a multiple of 5 is reached, the children must say "Hollywood." If a child says the number when he or she should have said, "Hollywood," he or she moves out of the circle. Here is an example of a game played without 5's, "1,'2; '3',"4",'Hollywood',"6",'7',"8",'9', 'Hollywood' (you don't say 10 because 10 is a multiple of 5), '11',"12',"13',"14', 'Hollywood' (there's a 5 in 15 and it's a multiple), "16",'17','18','19', 'Hollywood' (20 is a multiple)." Be careful when you get to 49 — the next 11 children must say "Hollywood."

Superhero Birthday Party

Every kid is a super kid. At this party, they can be superheroes, too, with their own superhero names, capes and masks. Make up a different alliterative name for each child — Mighty Mark, Keen Kate, Amazing Annie. Be warned! There's no telling what amazing feats your superheroes will perform after their party!

Red Mask Invitation

■ Purchased red half-masks, index cards, string, hole punch

1. Write the invitation on an index card, using Illustration 1 as a guide.
2. Punch a hole in the index card with the hole punch and tie the card to the mask with string.
3. Hand deliver the Red Mask Invitation.

CALLING ALL
SUPERHEROES!
It's time to
celebrate
Jumping Jessica's
birthday.
Sat., March 1
12 - 2

Wear this mask
to the party!

Supershield Invitation

■ colored construction paper, glitter writer, foil adhesive stars, fine-point black marker, #10 envelopes

1. Cut out a shield, 4 x 6", to fit the envelope.
2. Write the invitation on one side of the shield with black marker. Add each child's superhero name to his or her invitation.
3. Write the initial of the birthday child on the reverse side of the shield with glitter writer. Press on a few stars. Allow the glue to dry.
4. Mail the Supershield Invitation.

TERRIFIC TRACY

CALLING ALL
SUPERHEROES!
It's time to
celebrate
Jumping Jessica's
birthday
Sat., March 1
12 - 2

Decorations

- Make a red posterboard sign for the front door to greet the arriving superheroes. Use a glitter writer to write the greeting and to make stars and lightning bolts.
- Hang silver or red posterboard circles, 6" in diameter, from the ceiling of the party room. Decorate the circles with adhesive stars and the superhero names of all the children.
- Hang silver or red posterboard starbursts, 6 x 6", decorated with lightning bolts and superhero lingo: "Pow!" "Bam!" "Crash!"
- Use red and silver balloons and streamers.
- Set the table with a disposable silver table cover and red plates, cups and napkins.
- Write the children's superhero names on helium-filled balloons.
- Write the children's superhero names on helium-filled balloons. Attach the balloons to the chairs as place markers.
- Make a centerpiece by anchoring a bunch of helium-filled red and silver balloons in a foil-covered, 4" flowerpot. Decorate the balloons with adhesive stars.

Favors

Capes and masks (see Games and Activities), stickers, superballs, glow-in-the-dark lightsticks, small flashlights

Food

Powler Lunch

Superburger
Vegetable Villains
Shield Cake
Powl Punch

Superburger

Make one or more of these giant burgers depending upon the number of hungry superheroes. Each superburger makes four to six portions.

Ingredients: 1 pound ground beef, buttermilk baking mix, milk

1. *Shape* the ground beef into a large hamburger, 1/2" thick, 8" in diameter. Set aside.
2. *Mix* together in a large bowl 2 cups baking mix and 2/3 cup milk.
3. *Turn* onto a lightly floured surface and knead about 15 seconds.
4. *Form* into a large hamburger bun, 8" in diameter, and place on a lightly greased baking sheet. Bake at 400 degrees for 10-12 minutes, or until lightly browned.
5. *Let cool* 10 minutes. *Split* in half horizontally with a long serrated knife.
6. While the hamburger roll is cooling, *cook* the hamburger in a hot skillet or on a griddle. Top with cheese slices towards the end of the cooking time for a cheeseburger, if desired.
7. *Place* the hamburger between the two halves of the bun.
8. *Present* the superburger to the superheroes. Cut into 4-6 portions, depending upon appetites.

Vegetable Villains

The birthday child will be an able assistant in preparing these colorful, crunchy creatures.

Have a selection of fresh vegetables and fruits: broccoli flowerets, carrot curls, celery sticks, cucumber disks, apple halves and slices dipped in orange juice or lemon-lime soda to prevent discoloring, cherry tomatoes, melon chunks. Construct the Villains by connecting various fruits and vegetables with toothpicks or softened cream cheese. Present the Vegetable Villains with much fanfare and the superheroes might not even realize they're eating something very nutritious!

WELCOME SUPERHEROES!

cherry tomatoes

celery or carrot sticks

apple half

broccoli flowerets

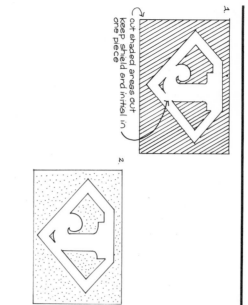

1.

cut shaded areas out
keep shield and initial in
one piece

2.

Supershield Cake

■ 9 x 13" cake, frosting, colored confectionary sprinkles, waxed paper, scissors

1. *Bake a 9 x 13" cake. Cool.*
2. *Frost with white icing.*
3. *Draw a shield with the initial of the birthday child on a 9 x 13" piece of waxed paper. At least two parts of the letter must touch the shield (see Illustration 1).*
4. *Cut out the shield. You'll need pointed scissors.*
5. *Place the shield over the cake and cover the cut-out areas with colored confectionary sprinkles.*
6. *Before removing the waxed paper shield, be sure no sprinkles remain on it.*
7. *Remove the waxed paper stencil to reveal the shield and initial (see Illustration 2).*

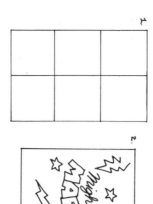

1.

2.

Games and Activities

Superhero Capes

These capes are guaranteed to be the hit of the party. Make them before the party and present them to the children as they arrive.

■ red plastic disposable table cover (104" length makes 6 capes); silver glitter writer or white craft glue and silver glitter; vinyl tape; foil adhesive stars; ribbon or yarn

1. *Cut the table cover into six sections as in Illustration 1.*
2. *Write each child's superhero name on a section of plastic. Use a glitter glue pen or write in white craft glue and sprinkle glitter generously over glue (see Illustration 2).*
3. *Decorate with glitter lightning bolts and foil adhesive stars. Let dry.*
4. *Turn over the plastic and lay a three-foot length of thick yarn or ribbon across the plastic, one inch from the top.*
5. *Fold the plastic over the yarn and tape with vinyl tape to form a channel (see Illustration 3). If you choose, stitch a channel on your sewing machine.*
6. *Adjust the plastic to form gathers.*
7. *Tie the cape onto a superhero.*

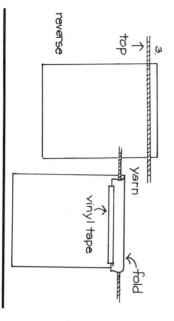

3.

top

reverse

yarn

vinyl tape

fold

Supermasks

If you sent Red Mask Invitations, the children can decorate the masks they bring to the party. Otherwise, provide one mask for each child.

■ half-masks, adhesive foil stars, sequins, markers, white craft glue

1. *Spread* newspaper on a work table.
2. As the children arrive, they can *decorate* their masks with the items listed above.

Making Monsters

■ Styrofoam® cups, assorted small plastic craft picks, google eyes, pipe cleaners, scraps of felt, fabric and ribbon, cotton balls, buttons, white craft glue, toothpicks, scissors

1. *Cover* the table with newspaper.
2. *Spread* the decorating items out and have the children construct monsters of their own design.

Superfeats

Ideas for Superfeats:

• Stand on one foot to the count of 10.
• Touch your toes 10 times.
• Balance a book on your head.

Award superribbons cut from construction paper to all.

Supersearch

The children sit in a large circle. Blindfold the first child and give him or her a wooden spoon. Quietly place a metal pie pan somewhere in the circle and slip a small prize underneath. Tell the blindfolded child to crawl around the inside of the circle hitting the floor with the wooden spoon until he or she finds the pie pan and the prize. Let each child take a turn.

Open Sesame

In *Ali Baba and the Forty Thieves*, Ali Baba opened the door of the robbers' cave with the magic words, "Open Sesame." In this game magic words will allow the superheroes to open the "Villains' Vault" (a foil-covered box, with the lid and bottom of the box covered separately). Select an adventure story to read out loud to the children. A selection from *Ali Baba and the Forty Thieves* about Morgiana, a clever girl who was Ali Baba's servant, will show a real superhero in action. Other wonderful award-winning stories highlighting individual efforts are *Once a Mouse* by Marcia Brown, *Swimmy* by Leo Lionni, and *The Emperor and the Kite* by Jane Yolen. After you have selected the story, whisper a different word from the story to each child. As you read the story and come upon the "magic words," the children will go to the "Villains' Vault" and take out their wrapped prizes. At the end of the story after all the children have used their magic words to open the vault, they may unwrap their packages.

Pinched Pennies

Those villains have been up to their old tricks and have hidden the superheroes' pennies. Give the superheroes small bags and let them hunt around the house for hidden pennies.

Music Activity

Play the theme from the movie *Superman* or other exciting music and have the children "fly" with their capes around the room or outside.

Teddy Bear Picnic Birthday Party

Everyone loves a picnic — teddy bears included! Invite your friends and their favorite teddy bears to play games like "Musical Bears" and munch on Bear Sandwiches and Bear-ly Punch. Too cold for a picnic? Not for a picnic you enjoy indoors under a tree you've made. Play the song "Teddy Bear's Picnic" and get ready for fun!

Picnic Basket Invitation

■ 9 x 12" yellow construction paper, 9 x 12" brown construction paper, lightweight cardboard, pencil, scissors, white craft glue, fine point marker, large envelopes

1. Cut a 9 x 12" piece of yellow construction paper into two 9 x 6" pieces.
2. Fold one 9 x 6" piece in half to make a 4 1/2" card.
3. Lay the card on the table with the folded side towards you. Draw a picnic basket; the fold is at the bottom of the basket (Illustration 1).
4. Cut away the shaded areas as in Illustration 1.
5. Glue together the side edges of the picnic basket and the two parts of the handle. Leave the top of the picnic basket open.
6. Draw the outline of a 3" high teddy bear on lightweight cardboard. Cut it out.
7. Use the cardboard cutout to trace a teddy bear onto brown construction paper. Cut out.
8. Write "Come to a Teddy Bear Picnic Birthday Party" on the picnic basket. On the reverse side of the basket, write the birthday child's name, date and time of the party, and a note telling the guests to bring their teddy bear or favorite stuffed animal.
9. Add eyes, muzzle, mouth, and ears to the teddy bear cutout. Insert the bear deep in the picnic basket.

Decorations

- Our Teddy Bear Picnic is planned as an inside party. It's fun to bring the out-doors inside.
- Decorate the front door with a big teddy bear drawn on posterboard or brown wrapping paper. Tape the strings of several helium balloons to one of the bear's paws.
- Create a tree for the picnic. Prop a 5-6 foot dead tree branch in a bucket of gravel. Drape green fabric over the bucket. Twist small pieces of green crepe paper onto the branches to resemble leaves. Tape Beehive Favor Balls to the tree.

Come to a
Teddy Bear
Picnic
Birthday Party!

1. 4½"   6"   cut away shaded area   fold

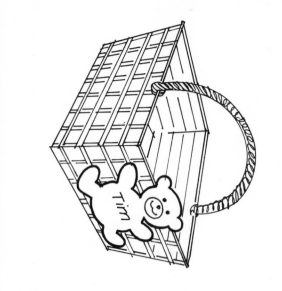

Beehive Favor Balls

■ an assortment of bear-related items to put into the favor ball: wrapped bear candies, bear stickers, bear erasers, bear jewelry or miniature bears; rolls of yellow crepe paper, tape

To make a 3- to 4-inch favor ball, you will need about 30 feet of crepe paper. Wrap the crepe paper as you would wind yarn into a ball. Every so often, insert one of the prizes into the ball. Use tape to secure an item if necessary and secure the end of the crepe paper with tape. Tape the Beehive Favor Balls to the tree branches.

- Draw a giant smiling sun on yellow posterboard. Tape with masking tape to a wall near the tree or hang the sun from the ceiling over the tree.
- Draw additional items from the great outdoors: clouds, birds, flowers, and trees. Hang them around the room.
- Spread a checkered picnic tablecloth under the tree. Check a party supply store for a disposable checkered table cover.
- Make miniature picnic baskets for the children's lunches. Attach pipecleaner handles to plastic berry baskets. Staple a 3-inch high brown bear with the guest's name to the front of each basket. Make extra teddies when you're making the invitations, and you'll have these on hand.

Favors

Beehive Favor Balls containing 4 or 5 of the following: wrapped bear candies, bear stickers, bear erasers, bear jewelry, miniature teddy bears (see Decorations), bear puppets (see Games and Activities).

Food

Teddy Bear Lunch

Bear Sandwiches
Berries and Melon Balls
Bear-ly Punch
Chocolate Bear Cupcakes

Bear Sandwiches

With a bear cookie cutter, cut whole wheat bread into bear shapes. Spread one bread bear with peanut butter and honey and top with another bear cutout. Put into a plastic sandwich bag. Place one or two bear sandwiches into each miniature picnic basket.

Berries and Melon Balls

Bears love to eat berries. Add melon balls for an extra good treat. Put several melon balls and berries into small paper cups. Add a plastic spoon. Put the cup into the picnic basket or serve alongside.

Bear-ly Punch

Mix equal parts of cream soda and pineapple juice for a fizzy, golden drink.

Chocolate Bear Cupcakes

Prepare a batch of cupcakes and frost with white frosting. Cover a cookie sheet with waxed paper. Melt a bag of chocolate chips. Spread the melted chocolate on the waxed paper. Chill the chocolate until firm. Cut out bear shapes with a small metal cookie cutter. Place a bear cutout on each cupcake.

Games and Activities

Making Picnic Scenery

As the children arrive, have them make an item of picnic scenery. Hang the drawings among the scenery you and your child have made.

Brown Paper Bears

For another arrival activity, give the children foot-high paper bear cutouts to decorate. Provide markers, crayons, glue and scraps of lace, felt, ribbon, wallpaper, or giftwrap. Hang the bears in the party room and let the children take them home.

Bear Puppets

■ paper plates, construction paper, crayon or marker, scissors

1. *Draw* a teddy bear face on the reverse side of a paper plate.
2. *Glue or tape* construction paper ears to the plate.
3. *Staple* the decorated plate to a second paper plate, concave sides together. Leave a hand opening at the bottom of the plate.
4. To use the puppet, the child *slips* a hand into the opening.

leave open

Teddy Bear, Teddy Bear

The children will have fun using their new Teddy Bear Puppets or their stuffed bears to act out the motions to the old favorite, "Teddy Bear, Teddy Bear."

Teddy Bear, Teddy Bear, turn around.
Teddy Bear, Teddy Bear, touch the ground.
Teddy Bear, Teddy Bear, show your shoe.
Teddy Bear, Teddy Bear, better skidoo.
Teddy Bear, Teddy Bear, go upstairs.
Teddy Bear, Teddy Bear, say your prayers.
Teddy Bear, Teddy Bear, turn out the light.
Teddy Bear, Teddy Bear, say good night!

Musical Bears

Play the classic children's favorite, "Teddy Bear's Picnic," for this game. Set up one fewer chair than the number of children present. In this version of Musical Chairs, the bears' owners place their bears on chairs as the music ends. One bear to a chair, please! No one leaves the game. The fun comes in seeing which bear doesn't get a chair.

Bear Charades

Bears can play charades — with the help of their owners. Each team (made up of one child and one bear) draws an activity written on a piece of paper. Ideas for activities are ice skating, taking a nap, cooking, sewing, playing baseball. The bear executes the assignment with the assistance of its owner.

The Bear's Picnic Basket

One child, the "bear," is blindfolded and sits on the floor near a picnic basket (or bowl or box) containing favors such as small boxes of raisins or bags of popcorn. The other children sit in a circle around the bear and must crawl to the basket, take out a prize without being tagged by the blindfolded bear and return to their spots. The first child the bear tags becomes the new bear. The game continues until all the children have prizes.

Buzzy Beehive

Toward the end of the party tell the children how much bears love honey and suggest that their bears might like to find some now. Have all of the children sit with their bears in a circle. Take one of the Beehive Favor Balls from the tree and give it to the child closest to the tree. Play music as the children pass the Buzzy Beehive around the circle. The child who is holding the Beehive when the music stops keeps the favor ball but doesn't open it. The game continues until all the children have favor balls — and it's time to see what's inside them.

Up, Up and Away Birthday Party

The great artist and scientist Leonardo da Vinci made the first model of a helicopter nearly 500 years ago. Two hundred years ago a French professor climbed into the basket beneath a hot air balloon and drifted for two hours above the trees. And in 1902 in North Carolina, Orville Wright flew a plane he and his brother Wilbur had built. Flying has excited people for years and years. Could you get excited about a party with flying games to play, kites to make and an airline lunch to eat? If so, let's go Up, Up and Away!

Helicopter Invitation

■ 8 1/2 x 11" typing paper, black fine-point marker, scissors, lightweight cardboard, envelopes

1. *Use* Illustration 1 for a guide and draw a copter design 4 x 4" on the card-board. Cut out.
2. *Cut* a piece of typing paper in half to make two 5 1/2 x 8 1/2" pieces.
3. *Fold* a 5 1/2 x 8 1/2" piece of paper to make a 4 1/4 x 5 1/2" card.
4. *Trace* around your cardboard cutout onto the front of the card to make the copter outline.
5. *Write* the party information on the inside of the card:

   Come Fly With Jacob!
   Flight Date: September 15
   Take-off: 1 p.m.
   Landing: 3 p.m.

6. *Provide* instructions on the back of the card to make the helicopter:
   a. *Cut* out the copter on the front of the card.
   b. *Cut* along solid center line to the dotted line.
   c. *Fold* down Sections 1 and 2 on the dotted line in opposite directions.
   d. *Attach* a paper clip to the bottom.
   e. *Drop* the copter and watch it twirl!
7. *Place* the invitations in envelopes and *mail*. Include a paper clip if you like.

Model Plane Invitation

■ inexpensive foam or balsa airplanes, fine-point marker

1. *Write* the party information on different parts of the plane.
2. *Assemble* the plane and hand deliver.

1.

cut

2.

1

2

fold

← paper clip

Decorations

- Make an Aviation School or Airport Sign for the front door. Attach helium balloons to the sign.
- Make airport informational signs to hang around the party room: Gate A, Gate C, Baggage GA, Baggage Claim-Lower Level, Airport Information, Ticket Window, Boarding Passes - Counter 1.
- Cover a wall with large sheets of butcher paper and draw a silhouette of a plane. Add windows, a "Jacob's Airline" logo, and identification markings. Or, draw the plane on a sheet and hang it on the wall. Line up pairs of chairs for plane seats along the wall. Attach belts, old neckties, or ropes to the chairs for seat belts.
- Suspend inexpensive foam or balsa airplanes and paper airplanes from the ceiling. Add balloons and kites, too.

Favors

Foam airplane kits, airplane erasers, bag kites (See Games and Activities), small toy planes, small parachute people, LifeSavers® Planes

LifeSaver® Planes

- rolls of LifeSavers®, sticks of gum, loose LifeSavers®, small rubber bands

1. *Thread the rubber band through the holes of 2 loose LifeSavers® (Illustration 1).*
2. *Hold the loose LifeSavers® and rubber band under the roll of LifeSavers®.*
3. *Lay a stick of gum, the plane wings, across the roll.*
4. *Pull the rubber band ends up and slip the ends of the stick of gum into the rubber band (Illustration 2).*

Food

Serve refreshments on "airplane trays" as the children are seated in their imaginary plane (See Decorations). Have a tray for each child large enough to hold a rectangular paper plate and a juice box.

Earn Your Wings Lunch

Wing Dings
Jet Pretzel
Vegetable Plane
Juice Box

Wing Dings

Serve chicken wings you've prepared or purchased from a fried chicken carryout restaurant.

Jet Pretzel

1 package dry yeast
1 1/2 cups very warm water
1 1/2 teaspoons sugar
3/4 teaspoon salt
4 cups whole wheat flour
1 beaten egg
Kosher salt, optional

Soften the yeast in warm water. Stir in sugar, salt and flour. Knead until smooth and elastic, 8-10 minutes. Do not allow to rise. Roll egg-sized pieces of dough into 1/2" diameter ropes. Cut into 3 pieces and form into a jet plane shape. Place on foil-covered, flour-dusted baking sheets. Brush with beaten egg and sprinkle with Kosher salt (coarse salt) if you wish. Bake for 15 minutes at 400 degrees. Makes 3-4 dozen soft pretzels.

Vegetable Plane

Fill a 3-inch section of celery with peanut butter, cream cheese or cheese spread. Place a 2-inch carrot stick across the celery to resemble wings. Make 4 notches in a carrot disk (see illustration). Use a little of the celery filling to attach the carrot to the front of the celery plane like a propeller.

Arrange the Earn Your Wings Lunch on a rectangular paper plate. Place on a tray along with a juice box. Add a set of "wings" made from heavy cardboard to which you have taped a large safety pin. Serve cake and ice cream at the table later on or serve balloon cookies with the meal.

Balloon Cookies

Prepare the dough for a chocolate chip cookie recipe. For each balloon cookie, measure 2 tablespoons dough onto the baking sheet. Press the end of a popsicle stick horizontally into the middle of the dough before baking. Bake according to directions. Let cool a few minutes on the baking sheet. Remove carefully to a wire rack to cool completely. Tie a red ribbon bow on the stick. For favors to take home, wrap the cookies in clear plastic wrap and tie with red ribbon.

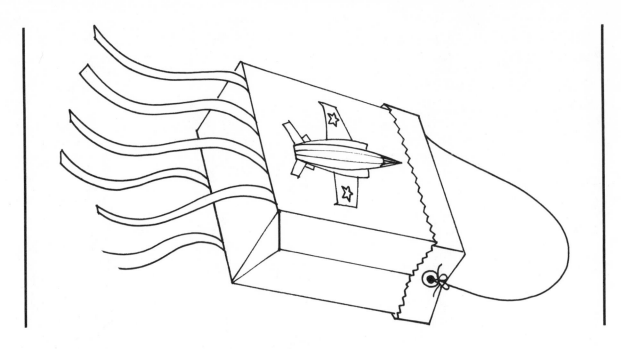

Games and Activities

Bag Kites

■ large grocery bags, markers or crayons, hole punch, paper reinforcers, string, crepe paper streamers, stickers

1. *Fold* down one inch of the top of the bag.
2. *Use* a hole punch to make one hole on each short side of the bag near the top and through the fold. Attach paper reinforcers on each side of holes.
3. *Tie* the ends of an 18-inch piece of string through the holes to make a handle.
4. *Decorate* the bag with markers, crayons, streamers and stickers as desired.
5. *Hold* the string handle and run with the Bag Kite — feel the effect of the air blowing into the bag opening.

Balloon Races

Give each child a different color balloon or write the children's names on balloons with ball point pen or indelible marker. Be sure to purchase balloons that are easy to blow up. Line the children up and tell them to blow up their balloons to the same size and hold them so the air won't escape. At the signal, "3-2-1-takeoff," have the children release their balloons. See whose balloon has gone the farthest, the highest, the craziest. The children will want to do this game again and again. Have spare balloons in case of mishaps.

Bobbing Balloons

Give each child an inflated balloon. Tell the children to toss their balloons in the air and to blow hard underneath the balloon to see if they can keep the balloons up. Next give the children a drinking straw and have them blow through the straws under their balloons and see what happens. Have the children try keeping the balloons aloft by blowing through paper towel tubes.

Paper Airplane Fly

Make paper planes ahead of time or teach the children how to make a simple paper airplane. Hang a Hula Hoop from a tree branch or in a doorway. The children take turns flying their planes through the hoop, first from three feet away, then six feet away and then nine feet away.

Before flying their paper airplanes, let the children try an experiment to help them understand how an airplane flies.

1. *Give* each child a strip of lightweight paper, 2 x 6". The child holds one end of the paper strip against his or her lower lip. The paper sags.
2. *Tell* the child to blow hard over the paper strip. The paper will rise. Explain to the children that air pushes on all sides of an object. When they blow very hard across the top of their paper strips, the air on top of the paper cannot press down very hard. The air below the strip can then push harder and makes the paper strip stay up. The same is true with a plane.
   A plane can stay up if the air below the wings pushes up harder than the air above the wings pushes down. A plane has specially designed wings which cause air moving over the wings to travel faster and farther than air under the wings. The air on top of the wings can't press down as hard as the air pressing up. This greater push upward keeps the plane in the air.

Runway Game

Make a "runway" with at least two turns. Use chalk on a driveway. Clothesline may be used on the grass or inside. Blindfold the first child. Tell the child to stretch out his or her arms like a plane and to listen to the instructions of the "air traffic controllers," the other children. The "plane" stands at the start of the runway and the "air traffic controllers" tell the plane to "bank to the left" for a left turn on the runway, "bank to the right" for a right turn and "proceed" to go straight. Each child has a turn as the plane.

Books About Flying

Read an exciting story about flying at your party. *Leonardo da Vinci* by Ibi Lepscky tells the story of the brilliant artist and scientist and offers much information on Leonardo's interest in flying. The 1984 Caldecott winner, *The Glorious Flight*, by Alice and Martin Provensen, tells the story of Louis Bleriot, a French aviation pioneer.

What's Cooking? Birthday Party

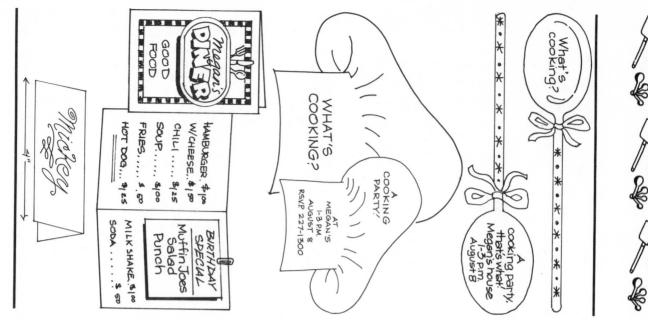

What's cooking? A birthday party, that's what! A guest list restricted to about ten children will let everyone have a chance to play chef. There's no need to plan too many activities for this party — cooking and eating will occupy most of the children's time!

Wooden Spoon Invitation

■ one wooden spoon for each invitation, fine-tip marker, ribbon or yarn

1. Write invitation on the bowl of the spoon (see illustration).
2. Decorate the handle with marker designs.
3. Tie a ribbon or yarn bow at the base of the bowl.
4. Hand deliver the wooden spoon invitation.

Chef's Hat Invitation

■ white construction paper, scissors, fine-tip marker, envelopes

1. Cut a chef's hat to fit into the envelope.
2. Write your message, using the illustration as a guide.

Decorations

- Hang a restaurant sign on the front door, advertising "Megan's Diner" or "Cafe de Megan."
- Create construction paper menus with your restaurant's name on the front. List meal selections and prices inside. Attach a "Special of the Day" card to the inside, highlighting the birthday party menu.
- Set up several card tables to create a restaurant atmosphere. Cover the tables with checkered disposable tablecloths and white or red dishes and napkins. With marker, write the name of the restaurant on the outside of white paper cups.
- Create bud vases for the tables by covering six-ounce juice cans with foil or red or white construction paper. Fill the vases with real flowers or paper flowers made at the party (See Games and Activities).
- Make formal place cards for the table. Fold a 3 x 4" piece of white construction paper in half. Use fancy printing to write each guest's name in red glitter writer or fine-tipped marker.

Favors

Food-scented stickers; erasers; jewelry and magnets shaped like fruits, vegetables or cookies; recipe cards explaining the day's foodstuffs; chef's aprons and hats

Chef's Apron

■ white fabric, grosgrain ribbon, scissors

The apron can be made from old sheets or inexpensive white fabric. Cut according to the illustration. You may use pinking shears or use regular scissors to trim the edges and stitch on your sewing machine. Write the child's name on the front with fabric marker or indelible marker. Sew 12" pieces of ribbon at four corner points as illustrated.

Chef's Hat

Paper chef's hats can be purchased at restaurant supply stores. To adjust size, take a tuck with a stapler. Decorate by adding the child's name with marker and adhesive stars.

To make your own chef's hats, you will need white drawing paper (18 x 24"), stapler, scissors, glitter marker, and some adhesive stars.

1. *Cut drawing paper into 9 x 24" pieces.*
2. *Accordian fold along the 9" side. Unfold.*
3. *Fold a one inch cuff along the 24" side.*
4. *Staple together to form a chef's hat.*
5. *Decorate with glitter writer and adhesive foil stars.*

Food

For this meal, divide the children into three groups and suggest that they wear their chef's aprons and hats. Each group will prepare a part of the meal. Set up three work areas and have all ingredients and utensils set out ahead of time. An adult or older sibling to assist each group will make the cooking simpler. Start the cupcake group in the kitchen before the other cooking groups begin, because the cupcakes must cool before frosting. The oven will then be free to bake the Muffin Joes. While the cupcake group is working, the other two groups can make paper flowers for the bud vases or play some party games.

What's Cooking? Lunch

Muffin Joes
Fruit Salad with Dressing
Sparkling Punch
Cake-in-a-Cup

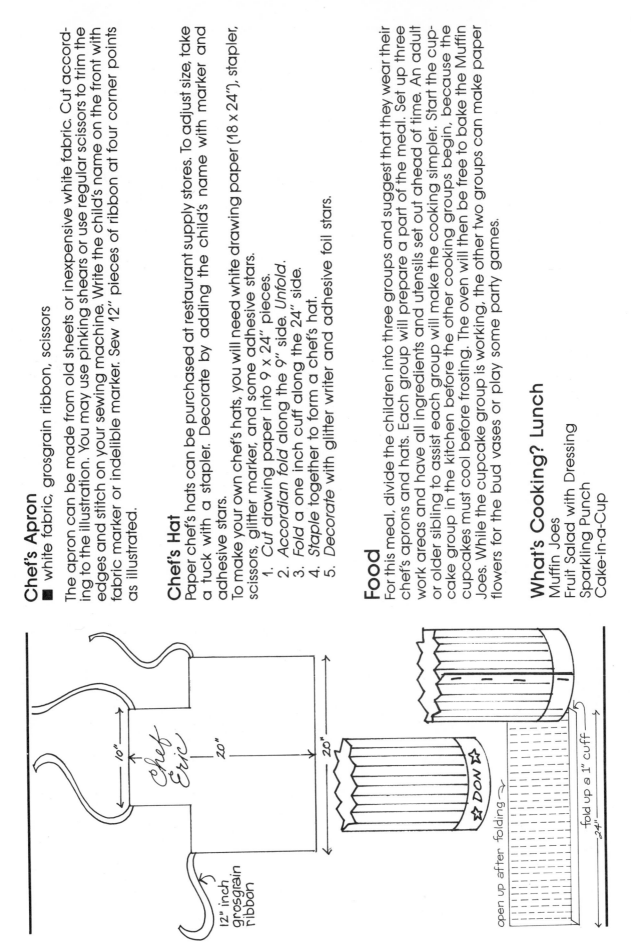

Food Preparation Area One

Muffin Joes

Ingredients: 1 can sloppy joe sauce, 2 pounds ground beef, 3 cans refrigerated biscuits (10 to a can), 4 ounces grated cheddar cheese

Prepare sloppy joe mixture according to the directions or use your own sloppy joe recipe with two pounds of ground beef. Place one biscuit in each ungreased muffin pan well. Press to form a shell. Spoon in two or three tablespoons of sloppy joe mixture. Sprinkle with grated cheese. Bake at 350 degrees for 15 minutes or until biscuits are light brown. Makes 30. For 60 mini-Muffin Joes, split biscuits in half and press muffin halves into wells of mini-muffin pans. Complete as above.

Food Preparation Area Two

Fruit Salad

Have the children wash and cut up various fresh fruits in season. Arrange on small plates. Serve with fruit dressing on the side.
Ingredients: 1/2 cup sour cream, 1/4 cup honey, 1/2 cup whipping cream, 1/8 cup orange juice.

Mix all ingredients together and chill until serving time. Makes 1 1/4 cups of fruit dressing.

Sparkling Punch

For 10 six-ounce servings, mix together one 12-ounce can natural fruit punch concentrate, partially defrosted, two cans water, and two 12-ounce cans gingerale or lemon-lime soda.

Food Preparation Area 3

Cake-in-a-Cup

Preheat oven to 300 degrees. Make your favorite two-layer cake recipe or prepare a cake mix according to box directions. Place 30 flat-bottom ice cream cones on cookie sheets or use 15 cones and bake remainder of batter in a cake pan for later use. Fill each cone halfway with batter. Bake for 20-25 minutes. Cool. After frosting, decorate with sprinkles, candies or dried fruit bits.

Games and Activities

Paper Flowers

■ colored crepe paper, green pipe cleaners, scissors

1. *Cut* three crepe paper scalloped shapes about 3" in diameter. Make a hole in the center of each shape.
2. *Lay* the shapes on top of each other, aligning the holes.
3. *Thread* a pipe cleaner through the holes.
4. *Bend* the top of the pipe cleaner to hold the paper.
5. *Press* the crepe paper petals up around the pipe cleaner to form a flower shape.
6. *Twist* on green crepe paper leaves.

The Chef's Alphabet

The children sit in a circle and the first child names a food beginning with "A." The next child names a food beginning with "B," and so forth. Don't forget quahogs and zucchini! A more challenging variation is to have the first child name a food, "tomato," for example. The next child must name a food that starts with the last letter of the previous word; in this case, "orange" would be a choice. The next word could be "egg." This game will keep nine and ten year olds thinking.

Wooden Spoon Relay

Have the children form two lines and give the first child in each line a wooden spoon. Place two bowls of peanuts at the opposite end of the room. The first child in each line must go to the bowl and scoop up as many peanuts as he or she can hold on the spoon - no help from the other hand! The child returns to his or her team and deposits the peanuts in the team bowl. The next child receives the spoon for a turn, and the process is repeated until all the peanuts have been transferred to the other bowl. When a team has successfully moved all the peanuts, they may share them for a snack.

Sniff Quiz

Select a variety of foods: lemon slices, crushed peppercorns, garlic, chocolate, cinnamon, and other fragrant edibles. One by one, the blindfolded children enter a room and sniff each of the foods. They then return to the party room and compose a list of foods they smelled, keeping their guesses secret. After each person has had a turn, all the lists are read. When the reading is completed, the host can display the foods.

Taking Your Party on the Road

There's nothing quite like a homemade celebration with games, food and invitations you've created yourself. But you may not always have the time or the energy to prepare a party from scratch. Happily, there's an alternative. You can have just as much fun by taking your party on the road.

Some restaurants and amusement parks specialize in children's parties, but you needn't limit yourself to those choices. You can build a party around any activity or excursion, whether it's watching a soccer match, taking a bike trip, learning about whales, or enjoying the ballet. The older the children, the more likely it is that they'll prefer this active approach to party-giving.

How many children should you invite? That depends on the ages of the children involved. As a general rule, figure on one adult for every four children between the ages of three and six. With older children you can get by with a ratio of one to six.

Buy invitations or make your own. You'll find ideas under specific topic headings, such as "dinosaur" or "sports" in the index to this book. Keep the food simple. Bring a brown bag lunch to the beach, eat at the museum cafeteria, or plan your excursion after lunch and meet back home for birthday cake when you're done. Add some favors and you'll have a party that's easy as well as enjoyable.

Now that you know the basics, here are some ideas on where to go.

Pack a Picnic, Take a Hike

If you're lucky enough to have a warm weather birthday, the only ingredients you need for a successful party are a park with playground equipment, some lively friends and a picnic lunch. For a winter birthday, you may be able to rent an indoor playground or gym.

Older children will enjoy a hike through a nature preserve or a ride on a wooded bike trail. Bring along individual bags of trail mix. Give compasses, magnifying glasses, Frisbees, butterfly nets or field glasses as favors.

Set Out on a Safari

Africa may be a little far afield, but you can always load up your car and head to the zoo. Call ahead of time and ask about special events. Many zoos have birthday packages, classes or private tours that can be transformed into instant parties. Cut out magazine pictures of animals to create your own invitations, buy hot dogs and bring animal crackers for dessert. For favors, give zoo guide books, animal books, balloons, molded plastic animals or notebooks with the zoo's emblem. To make your trip even more fun, turn it into a safari by giving the children clues and helping them find the animals that match your descriptions.

Tour a Museum

Whether you're fascinated by whales, computers, airplanes, art or the stars, you can find a museum to suit your tastes. Most museums now have "touch and feel" rooms or other exhibits and programs designed to appeal to even the youngest child. Some cities also have museums devoted exclusively to children. Call ahead for information on special exhibits and entertainment. If possible, plan a scouting trip to look around, pick up brochures to use as invitations, and buy unusual favors such as miniature dinosaurs or endangered species card games.

Spend a Day at the Farm

You can have a wonderful time going on a sleigh ride, a hayride, or a breakfast trail ride - or just horsing around on a farm. A harvest party at a U-pick fruit, berry or pumpkin farm can also provide a good excuse to spend a day in the country. Call the food section of your newspaper, your state travel bureau or your local farm association for the names of farms and harvest times. Draw a big apple invitation, pack a lunch to eat under the trees, and let your guests bring home all the fruit they can pick.

Be a Sport

Depending on the season and your interests, you can choose miniature golf, roller skating, ice skating, skiing, sledding, baseball, soccer, basketball or football. Don't feel you need to take your guests to a big league game. A seven-year-old football enthusiast will enjoy watching high school or junior college stars as much as the pros. Food can be as simple as hot dogs or peanuts at the ballpark. For favors, choose bubble gum trading cards, whiffle balls, and hats, pennants, pencils, notebooks or keyrings adorned with the insignia of your favorite team.

Make a Splash

What could be simpler or more fun for a summer birthday than a boat ride or an afternoon at the beach, pool or waterslide? Buy snacks at the refreshment stand and give beach balls, sunglasses or sandpails as favors. Be sure to invite enough adults to make it a safe trip, and don't forget suntan lotion and towels.

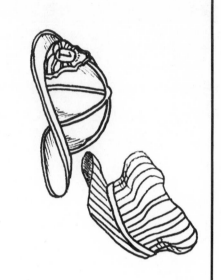

Plan an Excursion

Take your friends on a field trip to a fire station, police station, airport, factory or television studio. Many are happy to entertain small groups if you call in advance and come at a convenient time. Favors such as fireman's hats, police badges and coloring books will help your guests recreate the experience at home.

Or, take a bus, subway or train trip. The destination isn't as important as the ride itself, so you can stop just long enough for lunch, then take a ride home. Pass out maps, railroad caps or bandanas as favors.

Be Dramatic

Many community, university and dinner theaters have performances for children on Saturday or Sunday afternoons. Puppet shows, ballet performances, movies and children's concerts offer other possibilities. Make a paper bag puppet or ticket invitation. For favors, give finger puppets, autographed pictures, programs or the book version of a performance you see.

One last thing, parties outside the home can be expensive, but they don't have to be. With a little advance planning, you can schedule your outing for a free day at the museum, find a high school soccer game to attend or watch a rehearsal of a professional ballet company.

1, 2...Toddlers Have Birthdays, Too!

The ideal toddler birthday celebration, say many parents, is not a birthday luncheon for twenty children and mothers, nor a dinner gala for couples and their toddlers, nor a full afternoon of cake, ice cream and games for a dozen two-year-olds. Parents have found these celebrations sometimes do not turn out quite the way they'd hoped. Toddlers tend to be overwhelmed by too many people and too much noise in the house. A party requiring lots of attention to last-minute food preparation will take parents away from their birthday child and guests. Attempts at organizing a gaggle of two-year olds for a game fest are sure to be met with protests and tears rather than with enthusiasm and laughter.

So, how do you mark the occasion of your toddler's birthday in a special way without overworking yourself and overstimulating your child? A special celebration need not be elaborate. An occasion filled with love is the goal. Your child is the focal point—not the decorations, not the food. A gathering of the immediate family with cupcakes, a helium-filled balloon tied to the high chair and a brightly wrapped present for your toddler to unwrap *is* a special celebration.

Your toddler's older siblings would be delighted "to be in charge" of a family party. They'll find an afternoon's worth of activities in making construction paper party hats, drawing placemats for the family dinner table, designing birthday cards and banners and wrapping the presents. If you feel you must expand the celebration to include grandparents, godparents, other parents and their heir apparents, plan a gathering with easy preparation. Invite the family and friends to a summer gathering on the patio or deck. Guests can make their own sundaes or enjoy cake, ice cream and lemonade. For a cold weather celebration, serve warm spiced apple cider with spice cake or carrot cake.

For a birthday dinner celebration that will keep you out of the kitchen and with your child and guests, simply plan ahead. A week before the party make lasagna, cabbage rolls or another specialty and freeze. Thaw the casseroles and bake for the party. Serve buffet-style with a tossed salad, crusty bread and beverages. Make the cake ahead of time, too.

Toddlers in a party environment eat little. They'll be content to nibble cubes of soft muenster cheese, chunks of bananas, peeled pears and melon, and barely iced cupcakes. Serve apple juice in party-favor spouted toddler cups.

Make cleanup a breeze by using disposable table covers and heavy-duty paper or foam plates. Save the pretty ones for dessert.

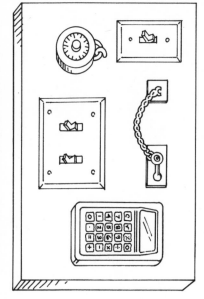

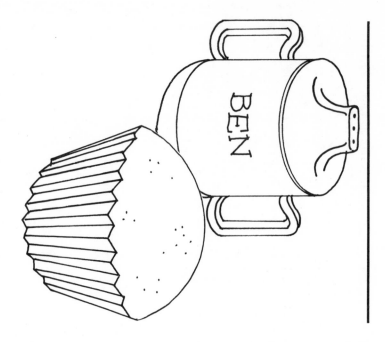

If your child is a member of a playgroup, the group may want to share birthday celebrations. Set aside a portion of the playgroup time for the celebration or plan a special outing to a nearby playground. The children will have nearly as much fun playing with party-favor sand buckets and shovels, small plastic cars or rubber balls as you will have taking pictures. Uniced cupcakes or soft cookies and juice boxes complete the party.

Homemade gifts are special for any occasion, but there is something especially loving in making a gift for your child's first birthday. Some families make a tradition of giving their children one handmade gift for each birthday.

One gift you can make which your child will find intriguing is a Hardware Activity Board. Another gift that will last for years is a Wooden Book.

Hardware Activity Board

■ 12 x18" pine board, 1" thick; sandpaper; latex or acrylic paint or polyurethane; paint brush; 5 or 6 hardware items such as a light switch, combination lock, chain lock, etc.

1. *Sand* the board smooth and round the edges of the board with sandpaper.
2. *Paint* the board in a primary color with latex paint or water-diluted acrylic paint. If you prefer, leave the wood natural and apply two coats of polyurethane. Let dry.
3. *Mount* hardware store or workbench finds to the board. Look for items that are easy to mount and which feature safe moving parts to fascinate toddlers.

Wooden Book

■ 1/4" thick board cut into four 5 x 5" squares (hard wood or pressboard); sandpaper; drill; water-based markers or acrylic paints; matte finish polyurethane; leather lace or shoelace

1. *Drill* one hole one inch from the top edge and one hole one inch from the bottom edge of each 5 x 5" wooden square, the "pages" of the book. Be sure the holes on each page are drilled in the same spot so they line up perfectly. (See Illustration 1.)
2. *Sand* the wooden squares smooth.
3. *Make* the book cover. *Draw* with marker or paint a simple object on one of the wooden squares. Leave room for a title, such as "Alex's First Birthday Book."

4. *Paint* or *draw* one simple design on each of the wooden pages. Choose items related to a birthday: a cupcake with a candle, a picture of a present, "Happy Birthday" written on a balloon, a "portrait" of your toddler. (See Illustration 2.)

5. *Brush* on two coats of matte finish polyurethane when the painted designs are dry. Let dry.

6. *Assemble* the Wooden Book by threading the laces through the holes and tying. Be sure to allow some "give" in the lace so your toddler can turn the pages. (See Illustration 3.)

Note: You don't have to be an artist to make the Wooden Book; the designs can be very simple. If you wish, you can cut out colorful magazine pictures, glue them to the wooden pages and finish with 4 or 5 coats of polyurethane.

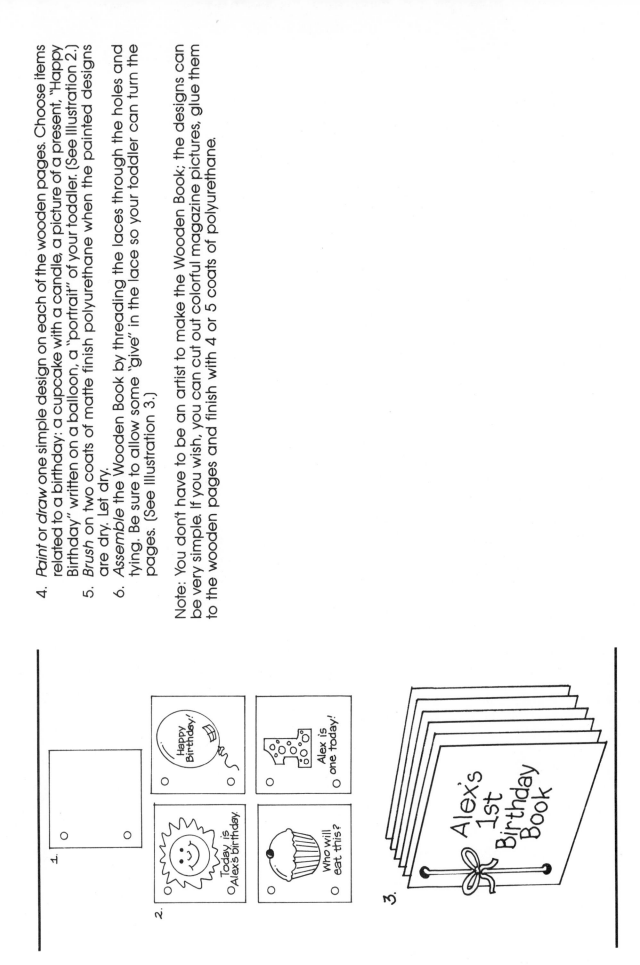

Celebrate Our Families

Family traditions bind us to those we love and help us learn what it means to be a family with shared values and a shared history. There are times when family ties can seem restrictive, but they also give us a feeling of belonging to someone and something which remain a source of strength and nourishment throughout our lives. Today, when many parents and children spend the better part of their days apart, it is even more important that we have rituals and traditions to bring us together. But we don't need empty rituals. We must find or invent rituals that are personal and meaningful and which encourage us to share in each others' lives.

If we choose carefully, the traditions we celebrate will teach our children the important lesson that love is a verb. Picasso said, "There is no such thing as love, only acts of love." Family traditions are acts of love.

Special Times, Special People

- Special people should have their own special flags. Make each member of your family a unique felt banner that can be hung on the front door or an outdoor flag pole to mark important events in each person's life. Birthdays are an obvious time to run up the flag, but there are many others: when Mom comes home from a business trip, when Mark gets his braces off, when Dad wins a tennis tournament or when Jessica catches her first fish. Making the flags can be a family project. Using each person's favorite colors, cut a two foot by three foot rectangle of felt, sew a two-inch hem at the top and insert a rod or dowel. Use glue to attach felt pieces, rickrack and trim to make a design. Include the person's name and symbols of their important interests. You might also want to make a family banner or flag that can be flown on holidays and other occasions that are important to the whole family.

- Make a family candle holder and have each person light his own special candle on birthdays, holidays and other important occasions. When someone is away, light a candle and say a prayer or express your good wishes for him or her. Use self-hardening clay and roll it into long strips to form your family's initial or something else you feel is symbolic. To make the candleholders, roll little balls (enough for everyone in the family) and stick the flat end of a pencil all the way through the center of each one, then attach the candleholders to the strips of clay.

- Make a combination greeting card and tablecloth for birthdays, Mother's Day, Father's Day, or any other day on which you want to honor a member of your family. Cover the table with butcher paper and let everyone draw pictures and write messages of love to the honoree.

- When you have visitors or a family member returns from a business trip or camp, put fresh flowers in their room and hide notes in drawers or under pillows telling them how glad you are that you can be together.

- On the last day of school, invite neighborhood friends to a picnic lunch in the back yard or at a park. Energy levels will be so high that you won't need organized games. Just be sure there's a swing-set, sandbox or playground equipment to play on. If the children are older, bring along a few frisbees, bats and balls.

- The first day of school is something to celebrate, too. German parents give their children decorated cones filled with cookies and candy on the first day of school. Start your own sweet tradition. Take everyone out for a sundae after school and talk about feelings, high and low points, new friends and new teachers.

Birthdays: Yours, Mine, Ours and Rover's

- Make a birthday placemat out of greeting cards received over the years. Arrange the cards on a piece of clear Contact® paper, and place another clear sheet on top.

- Celebrate family birthdays with an elegant breakfast complete with fine china, silver, milk in goblets, balloons and streamers. Serve the birthday person's favorite foods, perhaps an omelet with sausage or Canadian bacon, fresh fruit kabobs and a warm coffee cake with glowing candles. Presents from the family come after breakfast.

- Siblings sometimes resent all the attention showered on the birthday boy or girl. To make it easier on everyone, have the birthday child pick out something small to give his brothers and sisters when the presents are unwrapped.

- Welcome home the new baby and Mom with blue or pink balloons and a big banner. Brothers and sisters can pick out presents for the new baby in the weeks before the birth. Be sure that the baby also has presents to "give" his siblings.

Craft kits, books, paper and crayons make good gifts because they'll keep the other children occupied during this busy time. After the presents are exchanged, write down everyone's first impressions and feelings to give to the baby later on.

- When you have a new baby, you want the world to know. Put a pink or blue bow on the front of your house. Take Polaroid® pictures of baby, mount them on cardboard and attach a pin on the back for siblings to wear to school.

- Don't forget the canine and feline birthdays in your family. For Rover's big day, bake a spice cake and cut it in the shape of a dog bone, then ice it and inscribe it with his name. Family members can enjoy the cake while Rover feasts on a marrow bone, a scoop of cottage cheese, or cooked chicken livers. Present Rover with a new collar, a box of dog biscuits, a ball or a rawhide treat. Be sure to give him a bath and brushing before the gala event.

- For Kitty's birthday, bake a cake in the shape of a mouse for the family and serve Kitty a whole can of tuna fish with a candle in the top. Buy her catnip or a squeaky toy for a gift.

Moving Experiences

- Before moving to a new home, take photographs of the old one or have a house portrait done.

- As a family, write down the special things that happened to you while you were living in your house. Include the sad times and the happy times, what you liked about living there, what the neighbors and the neighborhood were like. Then write down some of the things you're looking forward to about the new house.

- Plan a friendship garden for your new home. Ask friends for cuttings from their gardens to take along, and transplant some of your favorite flowers from the old house to the new.

So You Won't Forget

- Keep a combination photo album and scrap book for each child that includes pictures of high points like the first bike ride, going off to school, accomplishments along the way, photos of friends, outings, and favorite places.

ALEX
7 lbs., 9 ozs.
June 15, 1986

- Give a present to yourself on your child's first or second birthday by starting a scrapbook of your child's art. Give the art titles, add the dates and glue the pictures into a scrapbook. The portfolio will grow thick over the years with wonderful drawings. You can also include your child's stories, poems and other creative expressions.

- Write letters to your children as they grow and keep the letters in a book to present to them when they graduate, marry or move to their first homes. Set a date for doing letters every year, such as birthdays, New Year's Day, Christmas or the first day of school, and write the date on your calendar. Talk about how your child has changed and grown over the past year, some of the important things that have happened to him, and what you like about the person he's becoming.

- Make a family recipe book that your child will treasure in years to come. Buy a blank book and handwrite recipes for your specialties, as well as those of other people in your family, and recipes that have been handed down to you from generations past. Be sure to include your child's favorite foods, along with comments about the origin of the recipe, special occasions when it was traditionally served, funny stories and other memories.

- Quilts are a wonderful way to preserve memories visually. You can make a family quilt with squares representing people, places and things that are important to your family; an extended family or friendship quilt with contributions from all of the people who hold a place in your heart; or a baby quilt to mark the arrival of a new member of the family. If you enjoy sewing, embroider or appliqué the squares. A faster and easier method, especially when children will be helping with the quilt, is to decorate fabric squares with indelible marker or fabric crayons. Back and bind the squares when they're done. Use the quilt the traditional way on a bed or cradle, or use it as a wall hanging.

- Vacation memories can be saved in a scrapbook that you take along on the trip. Collect brochures, ticket stubs, postcards and souvenirs during the day, then paste them in your scrapbook, along with your impressions, after dinner each night when you get back to your motel.

- Another way to preserve vacation memories and exercise your creativity at the same time is to make up a story as you go. Have the whole family sit down before the trip and decide what sort of story they'd like to write. A mystery, perhaps, or an adventure story? As you travel, be on the look-out for characters, settings and events. Add to the story each night.

Families and Extended Families

- Make a tradition out of providing each child in your family with undivided attention. If you have two children and two parents, you can choose one Saturday each month and divide them up. One child and one parent can go shopping, for instance, while the other child and parent go to the zoo. The important thing is to let the child pick the activity. Some families prefer to get a sitter for the siblings and let each child have both parents all to himself. If you're a single parent, you might want to find another family to trade babysitting with in order to spend time alone with each child.

- Involving grandparents in the lives of your children can be enriching for everyone. Ask grandparents to share their interests by taking one of the grandchildren to an art museum, going to opening day at the ballpark, or taking a class together at the zoo. Most children would also be delighted to go to the grandparents' house for a sleepover or share a picnic in the park.

- Surprise the grandparents with a basket full of homemade treats to celebrate a birthday or an anniversary. Make enough popcorn, cookies, and nut mix to last them several months, pack the food in pretty tins and boxes, then load them all into a large basket you've decorated yourself. Invite them to come back for refills when they're ready.

- Family gatherings are an ideal time to collect stories for a family history. "Interview" relatives and videotape or record their responses. Ask them to tell you about family heroes and villains, memories from their own childhoods, funny incidents, tragedies, achievements and recollections about family members you've never met.

Day by Day

- Create your own family holidays to celebrate events that are important to you. Dress in your best clothes, set the table beautifully with candles and serve special foods. To make a tradition out of your celebration, be sure you do it every year on the same day and at the same time, such as dawn or at dinner. Add games, songs, dances, stories and gifts, if you like.

- Are there people alive who haven't wished for an extra birthday or two, a day when they would be showered with love, attention and good wishes? Some families try to fill the gap by celebrating half-birthdays, but even six months is too long for some of us to wait. If you count yourself in the latter category, let each family member pick one day a month or every other month to declare "Today Is My Day." Write the day on the calendar and let the honoree pick out the meals, choose an activity for everyone to do together and ask for special favors.

- Designate one night of the week "Family Night," and ask everyone in the family not to make outside commitments for that night. Have a leisurely dinner together, talking about the things that happened to each of you that week, then spend the rest of the evening reading out loud, playing board games, doing a jigsaw puzzle, listening to music or working on a family project. Take turns choosing the activity.

- Choose a special tree or bush in the yard or a large indoor plant and designate it as the family "magic tree." Every so often the "magic tree" can bloom with a treat for each child, such as bags of popcorn tied with bright yarn, fruit roll-ups, sugarless gum, or small boxes of raisins. Let the children discover the surprises themselves.

Celebrate Our Friends

Sometimes we want to celebrate in a big way with a large gathering of our neighbors, friends of all ages, or our child's entire school class. The Olympic Party, the Come to a Carnival! Party and the School's Out Party will provide you with some new ideas for planning a gathering of friends and relatives, organizing a neighborhood block party or celebrating the end of the school year.

Many neighborhoods have long traditions of holding yearly block parties and feel these parties help form a special bond. It's sometimes hard to keep up with the comings and goings of the neighborhood. A block party offers a chance to sit back on a lawn chair with a glass of lemonade, renew old acquaintances and meet new neighbors, join in a rousing volleyball game, watch our children tackle an obstacle course, or sample tasty picnic fare.

Never had a neighborhood block party? You can begin a new tradition by working with one or two neighbors to organize the event. Start by inviting all the neighbors to a meeting to organize the day's activities. Set a date for the party and divide the work load—one couple may decide they'll organize a potluck dinner, a few neighbors may think running adult and children's games sounds like fun; another else will undoubtedly volunteer to hook up stereo speakers for music; another neighbor may want to organize a book exchange or white elephant auction of donated items. Send a flyer to each house well before the event. Include the date, schedule of events, items to bring, and cost, if any. Give several contact names so you can keep track of those coming. In few neighborhoods do all the neighbors know each other. Have nametags for the gathering and ask everyone to put their names and addresses on the tag; it will help in figuring out who lives where! It's fun to give awards at block parties—oldest and youngest awards, newest family, longest in residence, newest paint job. Make construction paper ribbons, decorated with stars and stickers. Set aside one or two yards for the games, auction, book exchange, or whatever activities you plan. Set up grills and picnic tables in a different area. Flowers from the neighborhood gardens make beautiful table decorations. Have the children decorate the block with sidewalk chalk drawings or a clothesline art exhibit of paintings done during the block party. Add balloons and streamers - and enjoy.

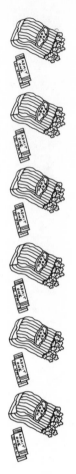

Come to a Carnival Party

Step right up for an activity-packed block party. Turn the neighborhood yards or a barricaded street into a colorful carnival! The games and food are guaranteed to please everyone in the neighborhood.

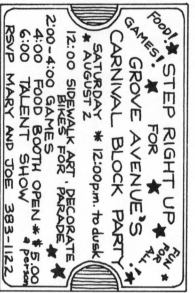

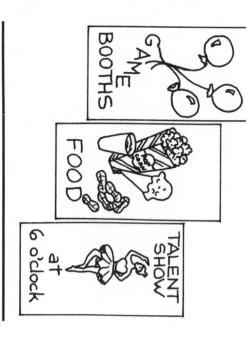

Committees

Get a few volunteers to take charge of setting up game booths and food booths, buying prizes, running the game booths, preparing and serving food, and planning entertainment.

Carnival Flyer

Photocopy a giant carnival ticket with the block party information. Deliver a flyer to all the families on the block.

Balloon Invitation

Write the block party information on small pieces of paper. Roll the papers up. Slip the rolled invitations into balloons. Tie the inflated balloons onto sticks and deliver one to each family on the block.

Decorations

- Make carnival posters to hang on houses, fences and trees. Have a poster painting party for the neighborhood children a few days before the block party. Supply large pieces of newsprint drawing paper, poster paints and brushes and ask them to paint colorful posters.
- Hang lots of balloons and crepe paper streamers along fences and from tree branches.
- Cover picnic tables with bright plastic table covers. For centerpieces, attach helium balloons to twisted paper sticks (available at party supply stores) and insert in sand-filled and decorated 46-ounce juice cans. Offer the balloons as favors at the end of the block party.

Carnival Games

Have volunteers make simple game booths. You'll need one or two adults to run each game booth and food booth. To add to the carnival atmosphere, the adult volunteers should wear bright colors and outrageous outfits - mismatched plaids, funny hats, and other festive costumes.

Game Booths

A card table or picnic table becomes a game booth when decorated with crepe paper, balloons, and a sign with the name of the game. You can also make booths by placing two chairs three or four feet apart and laying a board across the chair seats. Decorate with balloons, crepe paper and signs.

Some games don't need a booth (Bucket Toss and Bottle Cap Circle, for example). A sign attached to a fence or put into the ground will identify the game.

Game Tickets

Buy a roll of tickets (or make your own from construction paper) and give the same number to each child. To monitor the number of turns at each game (and number of prizes you need to buy), write the name of the game on the ticket. If you have five game booths, for example, you may decide each child will play each game twice. He or she will then receive ten game tickets—two for each game.

Carnival Prizes

Check the yellow pages for a novelty store that sells carnival prizes. Some stores package the prizes in smaller batches. If you can't locate such a store, party shops and variety stores are a good source for little prizes. Plastic necklaces and rings, decals, message buttons, erasers, pencils, badges, superballs, mini yo-yos, whistles, combs and stickers are carnival favorites.

The least competitive method of awarding prizes at the game booths is to give the same prize to each child for a particular game - win or lose.

Face Painting

A stool for the children to sit on makes face painting easier. Use acrylic paints and a fine brush. Acrylics dry very fast and the design won't smear. The paint is easily removed with washcloth, soap and water. Paint samples of the face designs on a poster and provide a mirror so the children can see their painted designs.

Mouse Hunt

Cut three different sized "mouse holes" in a large box. (See drawing) Children kneel about six feet from the box and roll three balls into the mouse holes. Scoring: smallest hole, 10 points; medium hole, 5 points; large hole, 1 point.

Ball Toss

A tried and true favorite. Draw a clown face on a large box. Cut out the eyes and mouth. Children toss tennis balls or bean bags into the mouth (5 points) and eyes (10 points).

Lollipop Game

Mark the ends of several lollipop sticks with marker. Stick lollipops into a foam cone (or into a flat piece of foam). Each child picks a lollipop. If the child picks a marked lollipop he or she wins a special prize, but all win a lollipop!

Bucket Toss

Line four buckets, one behind the other, with a foot between each bucket. Child stands two feet away for the first bucket and is given four bean bags. He must toss one bean bag into each of the four buckets. Award a prize for each successful bucket.

Bottle Cap Circle

Draw a circle on a driveway or sidewalk (use masking tape on the floor for an indoor game). Have the child stand three feet from the circle and toss ten bottle caps into the circle. Award a penny, peanut, or other small prize for each bottle cap winner.

Balloon Prize Game

Write the names of prizes on small pieces of paper. Slip them inside balloons and blow up. Attach the ends of balloons to poster board with tape. Hang the poster on a wall, tree, fence, etc. A child selects a balloon, pops it and wins the prize on the paper.

Fishing

Make small fishing poles with magnet hooks. Attach paper clips to sticks of gum, stickers, little rings and other thin, lightweight prizes. Put prize "fish" into a large bowl. Child fishes for one prize a turn.

Penny Drop

Fill a tall jar with water and place a smaller jar inside it. The child drops ten pennies into the jar, trying to get the pennies into the smaller jar. Award the child the number of pennies which dropped into the smaller jar.

Funny Fortunes

Write funny fortunes on small pieces of paper. Fold and put into the "fortune bowl." Children draw their fortunes. A few fortunes have a star, indicating the child has won a prize.

Magic Blocks

Float about twenty wooden or plastic blocks in a tub of water. Mark several blocks with small pieces of tape. If one with tape is picked, child wins a prize. A variation on this game is to mark the blocks with several different colored tapes. Each block will have a piece of colored tape. The children select one block. The color on the chosen block determines the prize, for example, blue tapes win balls, red tapes win rings, and so on.

Target Toss

Glue three boxes of different sizes, one inside the other, to create three target areas. Allow about six inches of space between the boxes. Prop up the boxes at one end so the target is at an angle. Have the child stand five feet away and throw five bean-bags, one at a time. Scoring: center box, 10; middle box, 5; outer box, 1.

Food

Select the items for your carnival menu and make a sign telling how many tickets each item costs. If you prefer, write the names of the food items on the tickets ("This ticket good for one ice cream cone," "This ticket good for one hot dog.") The children and adults can "buy" their snacks whenever they'd like and take their food to the picnic tables to eat. Or, for a more structured and uniform mealtime for all, "open" the food booths when you'd like to serve the food. Carnival food ideas: hot dogs, hamburgers, sloppy joes, potato chips, pretzels, caramel corn, peanuts, cupcakes, giant cookies, ice cream cones, soft drinks and lemonade.

Carnival Corn

12 cups popped corn
1 cup packed brown sugar
1/2 cup butter or margarine
1/4 cup light corn syrup
1/2 teaspoon baking soda
1/2 teaspoon vanilla extract

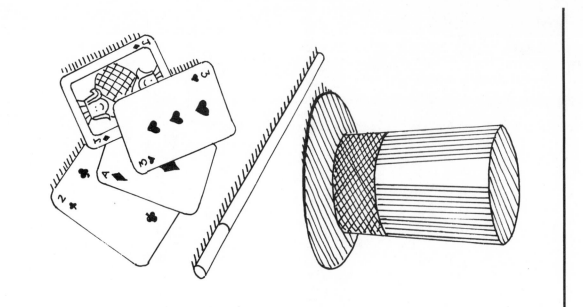

1. *Put the popcorn into a large roasting pan.*
2. *Combine the brown sugar, butter or margarine, corn syrup and salt in a saucepan and cook over medium heat, stirring until the mixture begins to boil.*
3. *Stop stirring when the mixture begins to boil and let it cook for 5 minutes.*
4. *Remove pan from the heat and stir in baking soda and vanilla extract.*
5. *Pour the carmel mixture over the popcorn and gently stir the popcorn until coated with the caramel mixture.*
6. *Bake the pan of caramel-covered popcorn for 15 minutes at 300 degrees. Remove the pan from the oven and stir the caramel corn with a wooden spoon. Return the pan to the oven and bake 10 minutes longer.*
7. *Pour the carmel corn into large bowls and let cool. Makes about 12 cups.*

Talent Show

When the kids are restless during the days before the block party, remind them of the block party talent show and have them decide on and practice their acts: singing a current popular hit, doing a gymnastics or aerobic routine with several friends, performing a few magic tricks, or telling some jokes. Encourage adult participation, too.

An Olympic Party

Archaeologists say the first Olympics were held around 1200 BC. and abandoned in 900 BC. The games resumed in 776 BC., the oldest events for which we have a record. In the tradition of these famous games, plan for your next block party to be a neighborhood Olympics.

Olympic Flyer
Make a flyer describing the day's events. Make photocopies and distribute to the neighbors.

Decorations
- Make flags of the world from construction paper or drawing paper and hang around the "game area." Neighbors may have their own foreign flags to fly.
- Attach posterboard Olympic torch cutouts to trees and fences.
- Cover the picnic tables in red tablecovers. Use white and blue plates, cups and napkins. Place small American flags and foreign flags, if available, in 46-ounce, sand-filled and decorated juice cans.
- Make nametags with a torch motif.

Setting the Scene
Decide at a preliminary meeting how the participants will be organized into competing countries. One way is to have the participants write their names on slips of paper as they arrive. Put the adult names into one box, the children's names into another one. Choose teams of about 6 by drawing names, so that each team consists of the same number of adults and children. The games are designed for children and adults to compete together. Have the teams draw country names, actual or fictional.

Next, have the teams design their costumes and/or flags for the Opening Ceremony. A large selection of various colors of sheet crepe paper, crepe paper rolls, large sheets of newsprint drawing paper, tape, staplers, stars, stickers, ribbon, and dowels (for flag poles) will become costumes and flags. Ideas: crepe paper sashes with stars, folded paper hats, or capes. Allow half an hour to an hour for costume and flag creating.

Opening Ceremony
After the costumes are completed, have the participants march into the "arena," the area where the games will be held. One participant could carry a torch (a flashlight with crepe paper flame). Play stirring music - Copland's "Fanfare for the Common Man," the theme from "Chariots of Fire," or "Rocky."

AN
OLYMPIC BLOCK
PARTY - AUGUST 10

SUNDAY - AUGUST 10

12:00 Help decorate
1:00 Team Selection
1:30 - 2:30 Make and decorate the costumes and have a snack

2:30 OPENING CEREMONY
The Competition

2:45 - 4:45 The Ceremony
4:45 Closing Ceremony FEAST
5:00 OLYMPIC Fest
6:00 Song

Cost - $5.00 per family
Bring an ethnic main dish
R.S.V.P. 383-1122

The Competition

- Make a big chart listing the participating countries. List the countries down the left side and the events across the top. Post in a prominent place. Fill in results as the games progress. Record totals for all teams or mark 1st, 2nd and 3rd finishes only.

- Play the games on grass to cushion any falls. You'll need a stopwatch and tape measure. Provide seating for those not participating in the games. One or two neighbors should act as officials to measure distances, time events and record statistics on the chart. They should not be competitors.

Gymnastics Events

Vault

Each team breaks down into pairs (for an odd number, one member participates twice). At the signal, the first two team members must "leap frog" from the starting point to a designated point and then back to the starting point. The next pair then goes. Each team continues until all have participated. Record times or record finishing order.

Beam

Give each participant a tongue depressor and a cotton ball. The first team member must carry a cotton ball balanced on a tongue depressor to a turnaround point, then back to the team. The next team member then goes. Continue until all have participated. If the cotton ball falls off the tongue depressor, the competitor must return to the starting point and begin again. Record times or finishing order.

Trampoline

Give each team a jump rope. The first competitor must jump rope/run from the starting point to a designated point and back to the team where the jump rope is passed to the next team member. Continue until all members have run the race. Record team times or finishing order.

Floor Exercise

The first team member must do a crab-walk to a point and a duck-walk back to the team. The next member then begins. Continue until all have participated. Record times or finishing order.

Rings

Line up each team. Give each member a toothpick and put a LifeSaver® on the toothpick of the first person in each line. At the signal, the first team member must pass the LifeSaver® onto the toothpick of the second person in line and so on down the line. Record the finishing times.

Horizontal Bars

Officials hold a clothesline 5 feet off the ground. Each team takes a turn doing the limbo under the rope. Lower the rope a foot for each round. Record the lowest level for each country's *entire* team.

Swimming and Diving

Freestyle

The first team member must get on his or her knees, use his or her arms in a swimming stroke (arms do not touch the ground) and move from the start to a turnaround point and back to the team. The next member then begins the relay. Continue until all team members have "swum" up and back. Record times or finishing order.

Backstroke

The first team member runs backwards with his or her arms doing a backstroke motion to a designated point and back to the team for the next swimmer to go. Continue until all have completed the relay. Record times.

Diving

Give each participant a clothespin "diver." Team members must toss their divers into a tub of water set six feet away. Total the number of successful dives (clothespins in the tub) and record.

Track and Field Events

Javelin Throw

Every competitor has a turn to toss a drinking-straw javelin. Add up each country's total distance and record on the chart.

Discus Throw

Everyone tosses a paper plate. Total each country's distance and record.

⬭⬭⬭⬭⬭	GYMNASTIC EVENTS	SWIMMING AND DIVING	TRACK + FIELD EVENTS
JAPAN			
ENGLAND			
DENMARK			
EGYPT			
PERU			
USA			

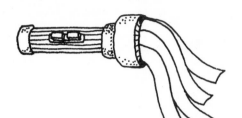

Shotput

Each team member tosses a water-filled balloon. Take the measure where the balloon lands or breaks. Total distances and record.

25-Yard Dash

Mark off 25 yards (or whatever distance you wish). All teams will do a crawling relay. The first member of each team crawls to a designated point and then crawls back to the team. The next member does the same, and so on until all team members finish. Record the times for each team.

Low Hurdles

Make a simple obstacle course of "low hurdles" — a card table, three-foot high rope between two trees, bamboo pole on two chairs. Teams take turns going under the low hurdles, one team member on the course at a time. Record times.

Closing Ceremony

After the competition, total the scores. Play patriotic music and announce gold, silver, and bronze finishers. Award all participants medals — a foil-covered chocolate coin glued to a cardboard circle and hung on a ribbon. Award small American flags and flag stickers to the children.

The Olympic Feast

Salute the countries that participate in your Olympics by planning an ethnic feast. Have each family prepare a dish of their ancestors' country. Have some families bring salad and bread, ask others to bring main dishes and a third to supply desserts. Ask the cooks to supply the recipes, and after the party put together a souvenir booklet of the Olympic Feast specialties for all the neighbors.

Day Is Done...

End the day with a Sing Along. Try to see how many songs from or about other lands you can sing. "Frère Jacques," "Waltzing Matilda," "La Cucaracha," and "Edelweiss" are a few, and you'll come up with many more.

School's Out Party

Invite your whole class to celebrate the end of another good school year and the beginning of Summer Fun! Or invite several families to join your family in a party to salute summer!

School's Out Invitation

1. *Take a piece of loose leaf paper and draw over the lines, using a ruler and a fine-point marker.*
2. With a ball point pen (so the line doesn't look as thick as the ruled lines), *write the invitation as in illustration.*
3. *Photocopy as many as you need and give to your friends.*

Decorations

- Decorate the back yard in symbols of summer — posterboard cutouts of happy suns, beach balls, baseballs, sunglasses, or flowers.
- Hang yellow, orange and red streamers and balloons from tree branches, fence and bushes.
- Arrange picnic tables and card tables (borrow from neighbors if necessary) or plan to eat picnic-style on the grass. Use warm summer colors, red, orange and yellow, for table covers, plates, cups and napkins.

Favors

Give everyone an inexpensive painter's hat and autograph each others' hats with fine-point permanent marker.

Make an autograph book for each of your friends. Cut typing paper in half to make 8 1/2 x 5 1/2" pieces. Fold 6-10 pieces into a booklet. Cut construction paper in half to make 9 x 6" pieces. Use the construction paper as a cover. Staple together or punch two holes and secure the pages with yarn or ribbon. Have your friends decorate the covers of their autograph books with markers, adhesive stars and stickers. Have an autograph session.

Food

So-Long School Lunch
Sloppy Joes
Chips
Frozen grapes, melon chunks and bananas
Lemonade
Brownies

WHAT I AM GOING TO DO ON MY SUMMER VACATION
1. Go with my family to the beach.
2. Sleep late.
3. Go to Megan's "SCHOOL'S OUT PARTY" Friday, June 10 3 p.m. to 6 p.m.
4. Read 4 good books
5. Do not watch too much T.V.
6. Weed the garden.

To prepare the frozen fruit, freeze small grape clusters, melon chunks and banana pieces until solid, about four hours. Serve frozen - a refreshing treat.

Games and Activities

Egg Toss

Pairs of children line up three feet apart facing each other. Each pair holds a raw or blown egg. The child holding the egg tosses it to his or her partner. After all teams have tossed their eggs three feet, the children step back, leaving six feet between partners. All teams toss their eggs, then move back to leave nine feet between partners. If an egg breaks, the pair leaves the game. If an egg drops, but doesn't break, the pair remains in the game. The game continues until one egg remains.

Note: For a blown egg, make small holes at both ends of the egg with a needle. Blow out the contents of the egg.

Water Balloon Toss

Follow the directions above but substitute a balloon filled with water for the egg.

Snake

Mark wide boundaries for the game and a home base about 10 feet square. Choose one child to be the Snake. The Snake starts off from its home to catch the other children. When the Snake catches a child, they hold hands and together catch the other children. All children who are caught must join the Snake. To be caught, a child must be touched by the free hand of a child who is on either end of the Snake. If the chain breaks, a new Snake is chosen and the game begins again.

Prooey

It, "Prooey", is chosen. Blindfold the other children and tell them to move around. Prooey stands still. As the children who are moving around touch each other, they ask, "Prooey?". Players not Prooey must answer "Prooey". The players keep moving about, touching and questioning each other. When the real Prooey is touched and asked "Prooey?" he or she does not answer but rather takes the hand of the player who has touched him or her. They stand quietly. Each child who touches them silently joins them. Blindfolds are removed as the children join the group. The game continues until all have joined Prooey.

Ear-sy, Nose-y
The children sit in a circle. Whoever laughs, giggles or makes any sound must leave the circle. It lightly touches the nose of the player on his or her left (or performs any similar action), who does the same thing to the next player. The action passes around the circle until reaching It. The next player starts a new action and the game continues until only one person remains.

The Number Game
The children march in a circle until an adult calls out a low number into which the group can divide itself. For example, the grown-up calls "three" and the children divide into groups of three. The children return to the circle and march until a new number is called.

1

3

2

5

4

Celebrate the Holidays

Holidays give richness and meaning to our lives. At their best, they help define us as families, as people with a shared history and a bond of love. They give us a feeling for the rhythm of life, and they help us celebrate the past and embrace the future. Unfortunately, holidays can also be times of great disappointments. We expect too much from these days, and we expect too much from ourselves.

How do you create holidays which are memorable and meaningful without falling into the twin traps of commercialism and excess? The first thing to remember is that you have a choice in how you celebrate. You don't have to send out hundreds of Christmas cards and bake twelve varieties of cookies just because you've always done it. You can retain the parts of your family celebrations that are satisfying for you, borrow ideas from other families and other cultures, and invent new rituals that are uniquely your own.

As much as possible, make your own celebrations, cards and gifts, and include your children in the preparation. The act of creating art, music, food or written expressions for the holidays is as important as the celebration itself. It also provides children with experience in giving and having their gifts seen as worthy.

This section of the book includes ideas for holiday traditions as well as complete party plans for groups. You'll probably find that some of the ideas can be used as is, while some will need to be adapted for your family. Whatever ideas you choose, you'll have the greatest success if you make changes gradually and discuss them thoroughly with everyone involved.

The Holiday Tree

There's one holiday tradition which is in a category all its own because its value isn't limited to one season of the year. The holiday tree is one of the nicest ways there is to mark the passage of the seasons, yet it's inexpensive and simple to make. The tree is decorated for each holiday: hearts and notes for Valentine's Day, shamrocks and Irish flags for St. Patrick's Day, jokes for April Fool's Day, bats and ghosts for Halloween, and so on. It can also be decorated to welcome someone home from college or a long business trip, to mark a special achievement, and to celebrate other family occasions. When there's a party or special event, the tree can "bloom" with favors or tiny gifts. Directions for making the tree follow. We've included suggestions for decorating it with each holiday. If you prefer, you can use a grapevine wreath in place of a tree.

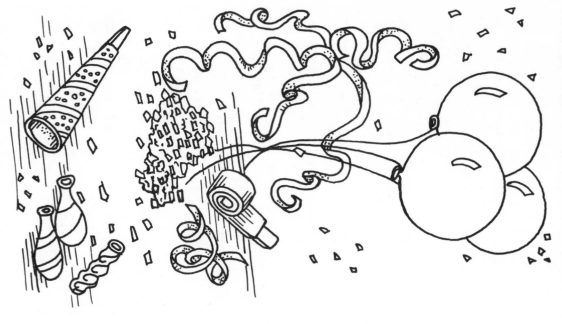

■ plaster of paris and water, 18" branch or branches with intricate ends like a real tree, empty 13 oz. tuna can, 15" fabric square, 12" wire or string

1. Mix enough plaster to fill the can.
2. Insert branches and prop or brace until the plaster is set.
3. Cover the can with fabric, tying with wire or string. Change the fabric to match the season.
4. Add a bow if you like. Use Christmas tree hangers to attach decorations or tie with yarn.

The New Year

The Muslim new year, Moharram, falls in January or February. The Hindu and Buddhist new year begins in the spring. People around the world may disagree about when the year begins, but for nearly everyone this holiday brings the same combination of nostalgia for the past and anticipation of the future.

Our new year begins in January, the month Julius Caesar named for Janus, the Roman god of beginnings and endings. Janus was pictured with two faces, one looking forward and one looking back, and a key used to close the door to the old year and open the door to the new.

As you close the door to the old year, what stands out? What are you most proud of, and what did you enjoy? Are there things about this year you're glad to say goodbye to? What are you hoping and planning for next year? Talking over these things as a family can open the door to rich communication.

- Many countries have traditional foods or customs which are supposed to bring good fortune in the new year. The Pennsylvania Dutch eat pork and sauerkraut. Southern Americans eat black-eyed peas. The Scottish people serve shortbread to the first person to set foot in the house after midnight. This "first footer" is supposed to be an omen of good or bad luck. Look into your own ethnic origins and see if there are any traditions you can adopt. Or establish your own "first meal of the new year" tradition.

- On New Year's Eve in Greece, children look forward to a visit from St. Basil, who fills their shoes with toys. The children are awakened at midnight to toast the new year with their parents and open their gifts. In our country, New Year's Eve tends to be a holiday for grown-ups, but having a family celebration early in the evening can help keep the children from feeling left out. Snip your own confetti and curl lengths of ribbon to decorate the table. Bring out noisemakers, and have everyone make a hat. Write fortunes like, "You will be called to be in a big movie," and put them in balloons to pop.

- Some families would prefer to stay home on New Year's Eve to avoid the crowds and the difficulties of finding sitters. Inviting the same family each year for a sleepover makes a nice alternative tradition. Bring out the board games, fix a crock pot supper, and make a ceremony out of writing your resolutions, putting them in envelopes and closing them with sealing wax, to be opened at next year's celebration.

- Holiday Tree: Hang pieces of curled ribbon over the branches and add family resolutions.

Martin Luther King's Birthday - January 15th

Parents who lived through the turbulent sixties have a wonderful opportunity to give children an eyewitness account of history. Share your memories of these significant years, the feelings you had about the civil unrest and the issues, as well as stories of people you knew who participated in marches.

- Documentaries on King's life and work, including his famous "I have a dream" speech are usually shown on educational television at this time. Make a point of watching one as a family each year. Afterward, talk about ways you can carry forward the dream of equal rights for all people in your own lives.

- Holiday Tree: Use ribbon to tie on slips of paper inscribed with dreams for the future and symbols of your dreams.

Valentine's Day - February 14th

Although this holiday takes its name from a Christian martyr named Valentine, executed on February 14 by the Roman Emperor Claudius because he cured his jailkeeper's daughter of blindness, most of the customs we practice today are thought to be related to the pagan Lupercalia festival which took place on February 15th. Goats and a dog were sacrificed at this time to ward off evil spirits and ensure fertility for women. But Lupercalia also came to be a special holiday for lovers. Roman girls put their names in an urn and boys selected names at random to be their partners for the Lupercalia festival.

Regardless of its ancient origins, Valentine's Day remains a popular holiday, perhaps because it is the one holiday devoted exclusively to friendship and love.

- Serve hearts for breakfast. Make pancake batter as usual, then pour it inside a well-oiled heart-shaped cookie cutter, set on top of a hot griddle. When the pancakes bubble on top, remove the cutter and flip them over. They'll retain their shape. Sprinkle with red sugar before serving.

- It's more fun to receive a love note than a packaged valentine. Write notes that begin, "What I love about you is..." for all your family members and hang them on your holiday tree or wreath, or hide them around the house in places like the medicine chest, the refrigerator, a dresser drawer or a shoe.

- Make your own valentines for special friends and family members. Some materials to use are construction paper, doilies, tissue paper, foil, ribbon, yarn, old wrapping paper, glitter, sequins and scraps of braid and trim - the glitzier the better.

- Holiday Tree: Hang hearts and love notes.

* Valentine's Party, page 127 *

Presidents' Birthdays

The birthday of our first president, George Washington, falls on February 22nd, although we now celebrate it as a federal holiday on the third Monday of the month. February is also the birthday month of another much loved president, Abraham Lincoln, and it is a good time to think about all the presidents, their lives, their times and their contributions.

- Although the story about Washington and the cherry tree isn't literally true, children have loved it for generations because it suggests that "the great were once like you." Bake a cherry pie, then read together about the early years of one of the Presidents. Make a tradition out of collecting stories you find dramatic or instructive. Did you know that in 1776, when couriers carried the Declaration of Independence to the people of South Carolina, it was nine year-old Andrew Jackson who was chosen to read it in the square of his small village because he was one of the few who could read? Jackson later became the seventh President of the United States.

- Holiday Tree: Make rubbings of Lincoln pennies and Washington quarters and hang them on the branches.

St. Patrick's Day - March 17th

You don't have to be Irish to love St. Patrick's Day. Patrick himself, who is Ireland's patron saint, was probably born in Wales, although he is claimed by England, Scotland, and France as well. Whatever his country of origin, he had a remarkable effect on the Irish people, being sent by the Pope to convert them to Christianity in 432 A.D.

His life reads like an adventure novel. Captured by pirates and sold into slavery at the age of 16, he went on to become a priest and bishop who baptized 120,000 people and converted the Irish people from their Druid beliefs. The shamrock, associated with this holiday, was used by Patrick to explain the concept of the Trinity, three persons in one God.

* Make a green banner for your door with the words, "Erin Go Bragh."

* Tint your milk with a few drops of green food coloring, then serve it with a meal of Irish soda bread, boiled potatoes, corned beef and cabbage.

Irish Soda Bread

Traditional Soda Bread:

6 cups plain flour	1 tsp. baking soda
1 cup buttermilk	1 tsp. salt

Mix all of the dry ingredients and make a well in the center. Add enough milk to make a thick dough. Stir with a wooden spoon. Mix lightly and quickly until you have a stiff dough. With floured hands, put onto a lightly floured board and flatten the dough into a circle about 1 1/2" thick. Put on a baking sheet and cut a large cross into it with a floured knife. Bake at 375 degrees for about 40 minutes. Raisins or currants are sometimes added to the dough for special occasions.

"American" version of Irish Soda Bread:

5 cups flour	2 tbls. of shortening
1 tsp. baking soda	1 cup of raisins
1 tsp. of baking powder	1 cup of currants
1/2 cup sugar	Generous dash of cinnamon or nutmeg

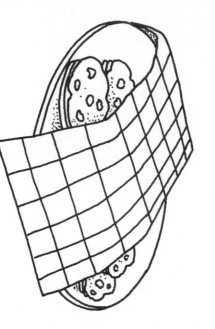

Enough buttermilk to make the dough stiff enough to handle. (About 2 cups) Mix the dry ingredients and add the buttermilk to these. Add raisins and currants last. When you are ready to bake, brush with milk. Again flatten the dough into a circle and cut a cross into it. Bake at 350 degrees for about an hour.

- For a living centerpiece, several weeks ahead of time, cut a sponge in the shape of a shamrock, wet it well and sprinkle it with grass seed. Keep the sponge moist.
- Sing "Danny Boy," "When Irish Eyes Are Smiling," and "My Wild Irish Rose."
- Holiday Tree: Hang shamrocks and Irish flags.

Purim

Purim is a joyous Spring festival which commemorates the victory of the Jews in Persia as told in the book of Esther. Esther was a Jewish woman married to the King of Persia who managed to save her people from Haman, the Persian prime minister who hated the Jews and wanted to kill them. On the day of the holiday, when the story of Esther is read, Jewish children write Haman's name on the bottom of their shoes and stamp their feet and yell each time his name is mentioned. It is a time of feasting and merriment for all.

- In Israel at this time, there is a custom called Shalach Manot, which means sending portions. Families bake together and make up decorated plates covered with white napkins. The children then dress up in their best clothes and take the plates around to friends and neighbors. The custom of Shalach Manot is also honored by sending money to the poor.

- Purim is also a time to stage plays that tell the story of the Jews in Persia. You can do the same by making finger puppets. Draw pictures of Esther, the King of Persia, Haman and other characters in the story on lightweight cardboard or construction paper. Cut two finger holes in the bottom and use your fingers for the characters' legs.

- Holiday Tree: Hang finger puppets representing characters from the story of Esther.

Easter

The holiest, most beautiful and most joyful holiday in the Christian religion marks the day Christ rose from the dead. Easter is celebrated on the first Sunday after the first full moon after March 21, but preparation for the holiday begins forty days earlier on Ash Wednesday. The time leading up to Easter is called "Lent" and it is a reminder of the forty days Jesus spent in the wilderness. Our name for the holiday is taken from Eostre, the Anglo-Saxon goddess of light, whose festival took place around the same time in the Spring. The symbols we associate with Easter, such as the egg and the rabbit, are symbols of regeneration and rebirth in many different cultures. Some early peoples believed that the world itself was hatched by the creator from an egg.

- Dye hard-boiled eggs or blown eggs (make a pinhole in each end of a raw egg, put a dish under it and blow until it's empty).

- You can buy egg dye in kits, but you can also make it the natural way. Simmer equal parts water and yellow onion skins for 5 to 10 minutes to make a golden egg dye. Strain the skins or leave them in for a speckled look. Mashed blueberries simmered the same way will make blue dye, grape juice makes a lavender dye, tea makes tan dye and carrot tops make green dye.

- For special effects, use crayons to make a design or write words on the egg before dyeing it. Dot dyed eggs with glue, then roll in glitter, or make speckled eggs by adding one tablespoon cooking oil to each cup of dye. For lots of colored speckles, dip in different dyes.

- Egg hunts and egg rolls take place all around the world at Easter, though few people remember that the egg rolling was originally a reminder of the stone that was rolled away from Christ's tomb. The most famous egg roll in our country is hosted by the President and the First Lady each year on the White House lawn. Have contestants roll eggs with their noses or carry them on spoons and race to the finish line.

- Another Easter tradition which comes from Greece is called "egg knocking." The Greeks believe that the egg is a symbol of life, but they also believe that you have to crack it open to get the blessings out. Family members hold their hard-boiled eggs with the pointed end facing out and knock them against each other until one breaks. The holder of the unbroken egg will have good luck all year. The loser gets to eat his egg as a consolation prize.

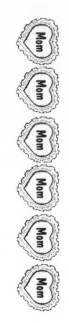

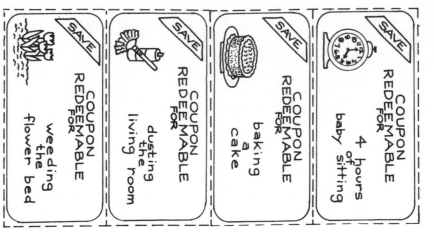

- Holiday Tree: Hang blown and decorated eggs or cracked egg shells filled with Easter grass and baby chicks.

* Easter Party, page 130 *

- Tell Mom to stay in bed and make her a breakfast of fresh-squeezed orange juice and Italian soufflé.

- The best gift you can give a mother is the gift of extra time. Are there things you could do around the house to help out? Make coupons for babysitting, dusting, gardening, lawn mowing or dishwashing and wrap them as a gift.

Credit for this holiday goes to Miss Ann Jarvis of Philadelphia who spent her life trying to have a day set aside to honor mothers. She was inspired by the untiring dedication of her own mother, who raised eleven children. Mother's Day was declared an official holiday by President Woodrow Wilson in 1914.

Mother's Day
☐ This section for Dads and kids only!

Italian Soufflé (Serves 6-8)

6 slices bread
1/2 stick butter or margarine
2 cups ham, cubed (1/2")
1 c grated American cheese or cheddar cheese
1/2 c chopped tomatoes*
1/2 c chopped green pepper

1/2 c chopped mushrooms
3 T flour
1 T dry mustard
1/2 T salt
4 eggs
3 c milk

*Add whatever vegetables your family enjoys - onions & zucchini are additional choices.
Butter a 3-qt. shallow baking dish. Trim crusts from bread and save to make bread crumbs. Spread the bread with butter and cut into quarters. Layer the bread pieces in the baking dish. Add the cubed ham, grated cheese and chopped vegetables to the baking dish. Mix together the flour, mustard, and salt and sprinkle over the

baking ingredients. Beat together the eggs and milk and pour into baking dish. Cover and refrigerate overnight. Bake uncovered at 350 degrees for 50 minutes. Serve immediately.

- Make a garden for Mom by planting a rose bush (or other favorite flower) on Mother's Day every year in a special corner of the yard you set aside in her honor.

- Write a letter to Mom each year telling her what you've enjoyed sharing with her that year, and why she's important to you. Keep the letters in a special binder.

- Holiday Tree: Hang pictures or symbols of Mom's favorite sports, hobbies, places, foods and family photos through the years.

Father's Day
☐ This section for Moms and children only!

Father's Day is a much younger holiday than Mother's Day. It wasn't proclaimed an official holiday until 1972. But unofficially, it has been celebrated since 1910 when Mrs. Joan Bruce Dodd, who had been raised by her widowed father, came up with the idea.

- Start the day with good wishes. Write a note inside Dad's newspaper, briefcase or lunchbox that says, "Happy Father's Day."

- Fill a brown paper bag with loving messages, and write, "It's in the bag, Dad," on the outside.

- For a supper dad is sure to love, make a hero sandwich by piling lettuce, tomatoes, onions and an assortment of cheese slices and cold cuts on French bread spread with mustard or mayonnaise. Top it with a toothpick flag that says, "Dad's a Hero." Serve it with chips or raw vegetables and a dip made of 8 ounces cream cheese, 1/2 cup French dressing, 2 tablespoons catsup and a dash of horseradish.

- After supper, present Dad with a plastic or rubber bucket filled with golf balls, tennis balls, fishing equipment, car wax and a chamois, pruning shears and gardening gloves, or other gifts that suit his interests.

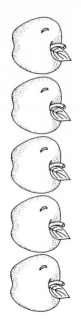

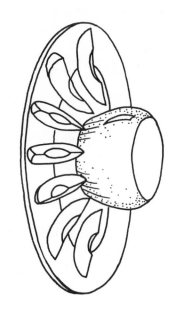

- Self-portraits and original artwork also make nice Father's Day presents. Mount them on cardboard backing or put them in acrylic frames.

- Holiday Tree: See Mother's Day.

Independence Day

The ringing of the Liberty Bell in 1776 that announced the signing of the Declaration of Independence was a significant event not only in our history, but around the world. Many other countries celebrate their own struggles for independence. Revolution Day in Russia, Bastille Day in France, Swiss Confederation Day and India Independence Day are just a few of these celebrations.

- Give a birthday gift to our country. Gather family, neighbors and friends and clean up a park, pond, stream or street.

- Holiday Tree: Decorate with miniature flags and stars.

* Independence Day Party, page 134 *

Rosh Hashanah

The Jewish New Year is celebrated on the first two days of the month of Tishri (September–October). It is a holy time devoted to prayer and self-judgment, and is followed by Ten Days of Penitence when everyone is expected to make amends for any wrongs done during the previous year. But it is also a time to look ahead and wish friends Shanah Tovah Oometukah, a good and sweet New Year.

- Apples dipped in honey are one of the traditional foods eaten during Rosh Hashanah to symbolize a sweet year. To serve, core an apple and cut it in wedges. Dip the wedges in lemon juice or lemon-lime soda to keep them from browning and arrange them on a plate with a pot of honey in the center.

- Make your own New Year cards out of construction paper, felt, stickers, and fabric scraps. Use markers to draw holiday symbols such as the scale, representing judgment, and to write "Shanah Tovah," a good year, inside.

- Holiday Tree: Hang construction paper cut outs of the Star of David and scales.

Columbus Day - October 12

When Christopher Columbus set sail on August 3, 1492, he wasn't looking for the new world, but rather a shorter trade route to India. When he finally landed on an island in what we now call the Bahamas, he believed that the brown-skinned people who met him were the people of India. He died never realizing that what he had discovered was not a new trade route, but something far more significant: the gigantic continents of North and South America.

In Mexico and many parts of Spanish-speaking America, this holiday is called El Dia de la Raza, the Day of the Race, because the Spaniards who sailed with Columbus intermarried with the people they found in the New World to create a new race.

- Columbus Day is a good time to think about the explorers of every age, from the American West to the Artic and outer space. Make a spaghetti dinner (Columbus was born in Genoa, Italy) and talk about the explorers' courage, their vision or lack of it, and how their discoveries affected our lives. What's the bravest thing you've ever done? What brave thing would you like to do?

- Take a family voyage to a place you've never explored. What discoveries can you make?

- Holiday Tree: Hang walnut shell ships with toothpick masts and paper sails stuck in clay.

United Nations Day - October 24

The founding of the United Nations in 1945 is celebrated around the world on this day. Part of the celebration is a collection of donations to the United Nation's Children Fund which was established to help provide food, shelter and education for children of every nationality.

- You can obtain UNICEF donation cans from your local UNICEF information office or by writing to U.S. Committee for UNICEF, 331 E. 38th Street, New York, New York 10016. Take them along on your trick-or-treat visits.

- Another way to celebrate United Nations Day is by focusing on a different country each year. Collect travel posters, read together about a country's customs and people, and prepare an authentic ethnic meal.

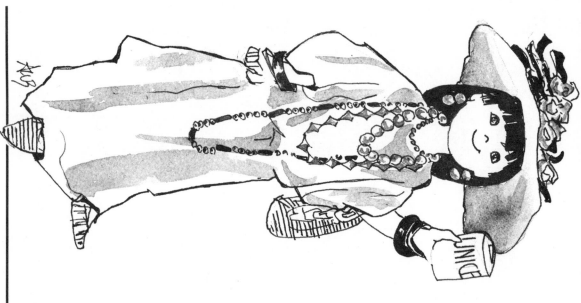

- Holiday Tree: Suspend flags of many nations or doves of peace from the branches.

Halloween - October 31

Halloween dates back to the Celts who lived in the British Isles and Northern France. According to the Celtic calendar, New Year's Eve fell on October 31, and that was the day they believed that the lord of the dead turned loose his witches, demons and ghosts. To appease them, the Celts lit fires, offered sweets and disguised themselves. Although the Christian church celebrates All Saints' Day on November 1st, All Hallow's Eve retains much of its pagan flavor.

- Most children delight in Halloween's spookier aspects, but some are honestly frightened by it. If you don't push them to participate, next year they'll be much bolder. This is a good time to talk about fears of all kinds, the ones parents had when they were young and the ones children have now.

- Take a trip to a pumpkin farm, and bring along cider and donuts for a snack. Buy pumpkins in graduated sizes for everyone in the family and do jack-o-lantern self-portraits. Then light the candles, turn down the lights and play "Symphonia Fantastique" by Hector Berlioz or the "Witch Scene from Hansel and Gretel" by Humperdinck.

- Create your own costumes for Halloween night. If you're not a good seamstress, you'll appreciate the ideas in *Easy Costumes You Don't Have to Sew* by Goldie Taub Chernoff, Scholastic Book Services, 1975.

- Holiday Tree: Hang up small bats and ghosts.

* Halloween Party, page 137 *

Succot

The Jewish harvest festival takes place in the fall and lasts for eight days. The tents or booths, called sukkah, which are built at this time are reminiscent of both the temporary structures that were built to house men laboring in the fields at harvest time and the tents which housed the wandering Jews after their exodus from Egypt.

- Families traditionally build a sukkah consisting of three walls and a roof made of branches and greenery with space enough between the branches to see the stars. The sukkah is decorated with fruit, vegetables and harvest designs, and is made large enough so the family can eat meals inside. You can cover the walls with sheets and have the children decorate a portion of the sheets each year by drawing fruit and vegetable designs in indelible marker. As the years go by, you'll have a patchwork record of your children's artistic skills.

- Holiday Tree: Hang construction paper cut outs of fruits and vegetables.

Thanksgiving Day

Harvest celebrations are almost universal. The Greeks honored Demeter, goddess of the grain, the Germans celebrate Oktoberfest, and the Japanese celebrate Kanto Matsuri. Our harvest celebration, Thanksgiving, first took place in Plymouth, Massachusetts. After surviving a difficult first year which wiped out half their population, the pilgrims invited the Indian chief Massasoit, who had given them corn to plant, and eighty of his braves to a feast of wild turkey, venison, geese, fish, cornmeal bread and succotash in honor of the successful harvest.

- Find out about the native Americans who lived on the land where you now live. What was their culture like? What foods did they eat? What games did the children play?

- Share your meal with others by asking someone to join your celebration, by serving a meal at a soup kitchen, or by making a food pantry donation.

- With relatives gathered together, Thanksgiving is a good time to take a family photo. Take it every year in the same place, with family members in the same positions. Once you have a collection of photographs, hang them together on a wall.

- Make jars of cranberry relish, tie ribbons around them and give them to neighbors as gifts.

- After the turkey's in the oven, play a game of football on the lawn or take a walk in the woods to work up an appetite. Talk about your family's history - how they came to this country, why they left their homes and what difficulties they encountered.

121

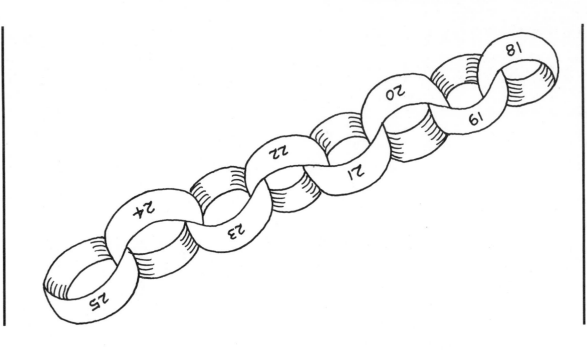

- If out-of-town relatives won't be sharing the day with you, stage a family slide show and include their pictures.

- Holiday Tree: Write the names of things and people for which you're thankful. Attach the slips of paper with orange, yellow and brown yarn.

✻ Chanukah Party, page 141 ✻

Christmas - December 25

Christmas, the day we celebrate the birth of Christ, holds a special place in the heart of each Christian, but it is particularly close to the hearts of children, who delight in hearing about the God who was once a child. Although many of the symbols we associate with Christmas have become misunderstood and commercialized, they originally stood for the light and hope which give meaning to this holiday. The evergreen tree, green through the long winter, symbolized everlasting life. Candles, which gave way to colored lights, reminded Christians of the victory of light over darkness. Even our much maligned Santa Claus is a variation on St. Nicholas, an early Christian archbishop of Myra who gave gifts to the poor and had a special love for children.

- The four weeks leading up to Christmas are called Advent, and there are many traditions associated with this time. Younger children will enjoy marking the passage of the days with advent calendars or paper chains made from construction paper. Advent wreaths, made from fir, holly or laurel branches are traditional in many homes around the world. The wreaths have four candles, one for each Sunday in Advent. Family members sing carols, read stories or say prayers as they light a new candle each Sunday until all four are ablaze.

- There is a growing movement today toward minimizing commercialism in Christmas and focusing on its original spirit. One way you can encourage this is by cutting down on the number of gifts you purchase and donating the money saved to a cause the whole family finds meaningful. With less shopping to do, everyone will enjoy the holidays more, especially if you add a new tradition. Hide the presents around the house and draw a treasure map, or write out clues in the form of Christmas riddles. In many countries, it's traditional to wrap presents with clues that suggest what's inside. A backrest, for example, might be wrapped with the message, "Here's something to lean on." A tag on a potholder might say, "Too hot to handle."

- Throughout the year, keep a book which the children can use to write down the things they'd like to have, then have them look through it before making a list. Writing everything down will take some of the edge off their desire and reduce pestering. Plus, children might be less likely to be influenced by the barrage of Christmas advertising.

- If you have a long list of relatives to give gifts to and don't want to resort to name drawing, consider setting a limit of $2 to $5 per gift. To add to the fun, make up gift categories each year such as "free and found," "old and rare," "something liquid," "second hand" or "something noisy." Encourage family members to shop at flea markets and garage sales, make their own gifts or give away clothes or toys of their own.

- Offer a Christmas performance as a gift to other family members. Depending on your talents, you might want to sing carols, put on a circus, do a puppet version of the real story of Christmas, or show baby movies of the grown-ups.

- Instead of sending out Christmas cards to everyone on your list, choose 12 out-of-town relatives or friends you haven't seen in a while, and write them each a personal letter. You could send one letter on each of the 12 days of Christmas.

- Whenever possible, make your own cards and gifts and encourage your children to do the same. Cookies, breads, jam, ornaments and other Christmas keepsakes, original artwork, coupon books, poems, letters and personal remembrances are always welcome at Christmas time.

- Make breakfast rolls, arrange them in the shape of a pine tree and deliver them to neighbors in time for Christmas breakfast.

- If cutting down an evergreen tree for Christmas seems like a waste, but you can't bring yourself to do without one, consider digging up and balling a live tree which you can plant later. Call a nearby tree farm to find out how it's done, but be sure to plan ahead since you'll have to dig before the ground freezes.

- Let each child choose an ornament each Christmas. By the time the children leave home, they will have enough for trees of their own. Be sure to write the date on the back in indelible marker. This is also a nice tradition for a grandparent who might like to give an ornament to each child as a gift each year.

"Jessica would like....."

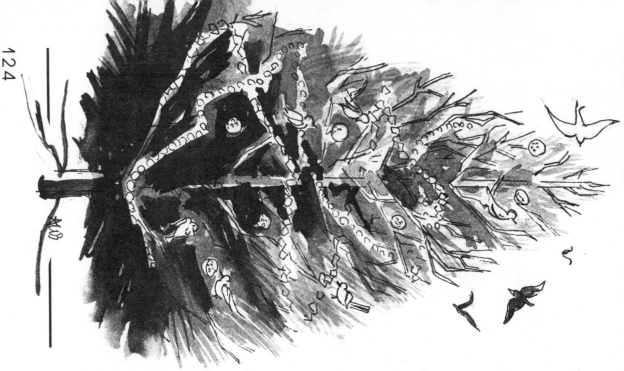

- Have a tree-trimming party. Serve hot cocoa and cookies, string popcorn or make paper chains, and sing carols.

- On Christmas Eve, line the walk leading to your home with luminaria. Fill lunch bags about half-full with sand and stick a candle in each one. Vigil candles work well. The sand will keep the candles from falling over and will snuff them out when they burn down.

- Just before going to bed on Christmas Eve, gather around the Christmas tree, turn off all but the tree lights and sing carols. Have the youngest children join in by playing a xylophone or jingle bells. At the end, have someone in the family tell or read the real story of Christmas and sing "Silent Night."

- Christmas is one holiday in which animals play an unusually important role. The oxen and the sheep were among the few on earth that were privileged to witness the birth of Christ. This fact has inspired many beautiful traditions. St. Francis of Assisi wanted "all creation" to share in the joy of Christmas, so he gave farm animals an extra helping of food at this time. In the Scandinavian countries, sheaves of wheat are placed on roofs and poles for the birds, and bits of suet are fastened to trees. In Northern Europe, children put out food for St. Nicholas' white horse, and in Spain, they put out hay for the Three Kings' camels. There is also a legend that animals are given the gift of speech on Christmas Eve so that they can tell the glad tidings. One nice way to create a feast for the animals is to move your Christmas tree out to the yard after the decorations are removed and decorate it with strings of cranberries and hollowed out orange halves filled with ground suet and bird seed.

- In Great Britain, the day after Christmas is a holiday called Boxing Day. It's a time when everyone, including the king and queen, box up food, toys and clothes to give to the poor. Instead of fighting the crowds of shoppers at after-Christmas sales, stay home and gather together the things you no longer need that others might find useful.

- Epiphany is an important holiday in Mexico, Columbia, Argentina and other parts of Spanish-speaking America. It is called El Dia de Reyes, Three Kings Day, and marks the time when Melchior, Kaspar and Balthasar followed the star to Bethlehem, where Jesus was born. Mexican children leave their shoes on the window in hopes that the three kings will fill them with candy, fruit and toys. They also leave water for the kings' camels. In the afternoon, family members gather to eat "Three Kings Cake." To make one for your family, bake a cake in a ring shape to resemble a crown, using a Bundt pan or angel food cake pan. Add surprises for the children to the cake batter. Wrap them in foil if you wish. Bake them right along with the cake. After it's frosted, decorate it with candied cherry and pineapple "jewels."

- Holiday Tree: Decorate with ornaments, cards or gingerbread men.

* Christmas Party, page 144 *

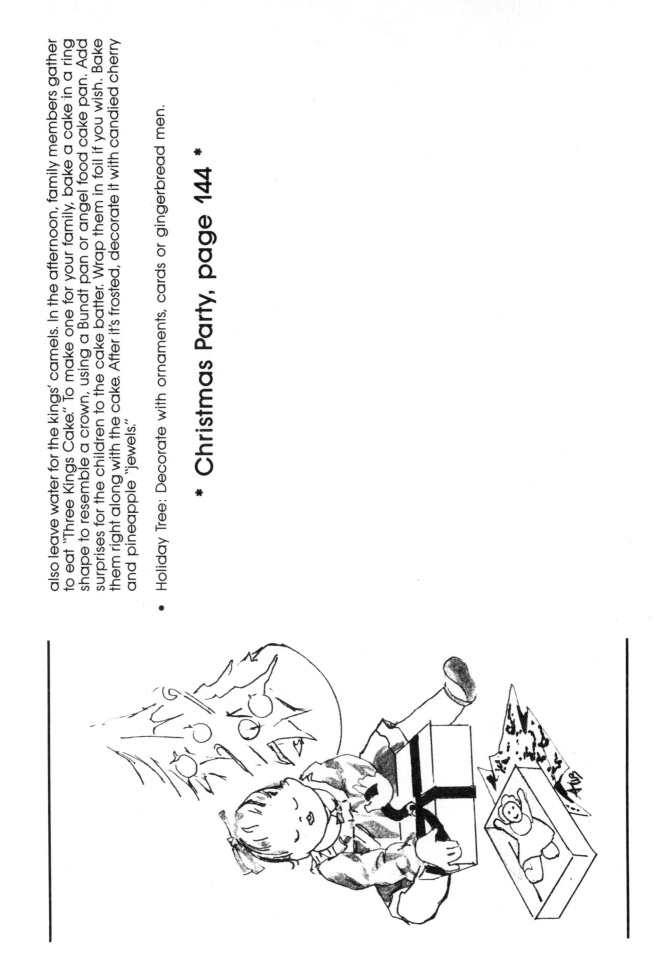

Valentine's Day Party

Celebrate friendship! Invite some pals over to trade valentines. Don't forget to ask them to dress in red.

Pop-Up Invitations

- 9 x 12" red and white construction paper, red marker, glue, 6 x 9" envelopes

1. *Cut* a piece of red construction paper in half to make two 6 x 9" pieces.
2. *Fold* the pieces in half to make two cards.
3. *Cut* another strip of red paper, about 1 x 4", and *fold* it, accordion-style.
4. *Cut* out a small white heart, 3 x 4".
5. *Glue* one end of the folded strip of paper inside the card, and glue the heart to the other end.
6. *Write* the invitation on the heart, put it in an envelope and mail.

Decorations

- Hang red and white crepe paper and balloons.
- Cut out hearts from construction paper and inscribe them with messages, such as "Be Mine," and "I Love You." Hang them around the house.
- Use red napkins and tablecloth, with large white doilies for place mats.
- Place a heart cake (see Food) on a doily for the centerpiece.
- Make heart mobiles by cutting out construction paper hearts in graduated sizes and taping them on white satin or curled ribbon. You can also make a "Valentine person" from ribbons and hearts.

Favors

Candy hearts, valentines, stickers, heart erasers, heart pencils, heart pins or barrettes, red rubber balls, claybake heart necklaces (see Games and Activities)

Food

Cupid's Feast
Valentine Sandwiches
Apple Hearts
Heart Cake
Love Potion Float

Valentine Sandwiches
Cut heart-shaped pieces of bread with a cookie cutter and spread with peanut butter or cream cheese topped with strawberry jam.

Love you to have you come to my Valentine Party

Jessica's House,
1350 N. East,
Saturday,
February 14th
1 - 3 p.m.

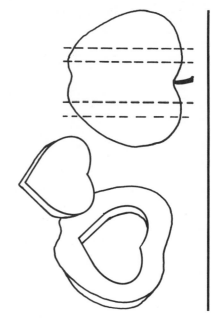

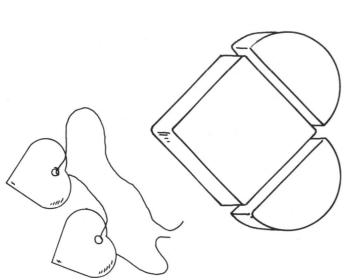

Apple Hearts

Cut two slices (top to bottom) from each side of a red delicious apple. Then use a small metal cookie cutter to cut out a heart from the center of each slice. Dip the pieces in lemon-lime soda or lemon juice to keep them from turning brown. Serve both pieces of apple so the children can use them as puzzles.

Heart Cake

Use your favorite two-layer recipe or a standard cake mix and bake in one square and one round pan. Make sure the pans are the same size — each eight-inch or each nine-inch. When cool, cut the round layer in half and place the halves against two adjacent sides of the square layer to form a heart. Frost with pink or white frosting. Add a border of red cinnamon candies or a sprinkling of red sugar.

Love Potion Float

Float raspberry sherbet scoops made with a melon baller in cranberry juice.

Games and Activities

Claybake Necklaces

4 cups flour
1 cup plain or iodized salt
1 1/2 cups hot tap water
food coloring to tint dough

Pour hot water, food coloring and salt into a bowl and stir for one minute. The grains of salt will diminish in size, but will not dissolve. Add the flour. Stir until all water is absorbed. Turn dough onto the table or a bread board and knead a few minutes. Dough is ready when it's smooth and pliable. Roll out 1/4" thick and cut with a heart cookie cutter. Poke a hole in the top with a drinking straw. Bake at 200 degrees for one hour. When cool, thread the hearts on red yarn or ribbon to make necklaces.

Post Office

Decorate a box with marker or crayon, construction paper hearts, doilies and stickers, then put a slit in the top to make a "mail box." Buy a large box of inexpensive valentines or have the children make their own out of scraps and "mail" them. Just before going home, open the mail box and distribute the valentines, making sure that everyone gets some.

The Missing Pieces of My Heart

Cut construction paper hearts in half so that no two pairs are alike. Each child must find the child whose piece completes his or her half. The children whose hearts match will be partners for the next game.

Silly Balloons

Inflate red and white balloons for each child, and decorate them with marking pen hearts. Insert a marble into the neck of each balloon before you blow it up. Partners must toss a balloon back and forth, taking a step back each time to make it a challenge. The balloons will zigzag in the air, making them difficult to catch. A variation is to give a balloon to each child and tell them to try to keep it in the air, without letting it touch the floor.

Clothesline Game

■ two pairs of scissors, red construction paper, crayons or stickers, spring clothespins, clothesline

Hang a clothesline across the room. Form two lines. The first child in each team cuts out a valentine from construction paper, writes the name of the child behind him or her (or puts a sticker on it if too young to write), runs to the clothesline and hangs it up. Then the next person in line pins one up, and so on until all children have hung their valentines.

What's Missing

Fill a tray with Valentine's Day items such as candy hearts with messages, doilies, flowers, an ace of hearts, and heart cookie cutters. Remove items while the children close their eyes and have them guess what's missing.

Easter Brunch

Organize an Easter brunch and you may find you've started a yearly tradition. Invite your family or wake the neighborhood for an Easter egg hunt at dawn.

Hop Over
to
Mark's
for
Easter Brunch
Sunday
March 30
10 to 1

Molly

R.S.V.P.
000-0000

Invitation

▪ pink construction paper, white yarn, cotton balls, marker or crayon, glue

1. Cut out a bunny silhouette, about 4 x 6" from construction paper.
2. Draw a face and whiskers (or use bits of yarn) and write the invitation on the front.
3. Glue a cotton-ball tail on the reverse side.

Decorations

• Decorate the bare branches of a bush in front of your house with brightly colored plastic eggs. (Buy them or save hosiery containers and decorate with stickers.)
• Place stuffed bunnies and chicks around the house. Let them peek out from behind chairs, nestle in plants or sit on the window sill.
• Use spring colors, pink, yellow, green, and lavender, for streamers and balloon bouquets.
• Set the table with purple and yellow tablecloth, napkins, plates, and cups.
• Set an Easter basket full of colored eggs and real grass in the center of the table.
• For place cards, write each guest's name in crayon on an egg before dyeing it. Make a stand by cutting a one-inch ring from an empty paper towel or toilet paper tube, covering it with construction paper, and decorating it with stickers or markers.

Favors

To cut down on the number of jelly beans and chocolate eggs without ruining your Easter egg hunt, fill plastic hosiery containers or eggs with inexpensive toys, trinkets, jewelry, stickers, or pennies. Sandpails make attractive recyclable Easter baskets. You can also use plastic watering cans or flowerpots filled with packets of seeds or children's gardening tools.

Food
Easter Brunch
Hide n' Seek Eggs
Bunny Salad
Orange Delights
Bunny Cake

Hide n' Seek Eggs

2 tubes crescent rolls (8 to a tube)
4 hard-boiled eggs
8 thin slices ham
8 thin slices Swiss cheese

Preheat oven to 400 degrees. Pinch together 2 crescent triangles to form a rectangle. Place a slice of ham and a slice of cheese on the dough, trimming ham and cheese to fit. Place half a hard-boiled egg at one of the narrow ends of the dough. Beginning at egg end, roll up with the egg inside. Pinch dough at both ends, and fold under so that all three seams are on the bottom. Brush with milk or beaten egg. Sprinkle with sesame seeds or poppy seeds. Place on a lightly greased cookie sheet. Bake for 10-12 minutes, until golden. Serves 8.

Bunny Salad

6 canned pear halves
3 ounces cheddar cheese
1/4 cup raisins

6 radishes
lettuce

For each bunny, place one pear half on a bed of lettuce as shown. Use raisins to make eyes, radish bits to make nose and mouth, and cheese slices for ears. Make slits in the pear to hold features in place.

Orange Delights

1 1/2 cups orange juice
1 1/2 cups milk
1 1/2 cups crushed ice
1 teaspoon vanilla extract

Place all ingredients in a blender and mix well. Serves 6.

Bunny Cake

Bake a cake recipe in two round pans and cut each cake in half. Line up three of the halves, standing on the cut edge, on a plate. Cut a face and ears from the remaining half and put in front of the three layers (Illustration 1). Ice and decorate. Alternately, place one whole cake on a cookie sheet. Cut ears and bow tie out of second layer (Illustration 2). Ice with white, pink, and yellow frosting. Decorate with coconut and use jelly beans to make eyes and nose (Illustration 3).

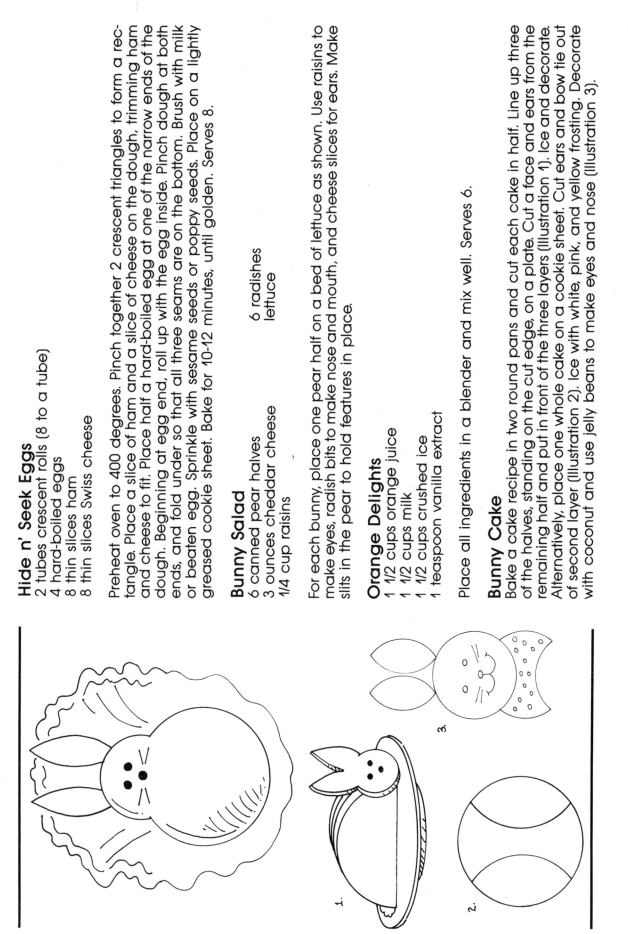

131

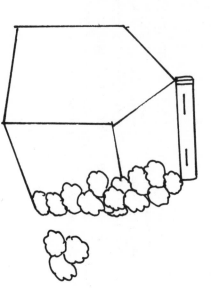

Games and Activities

Bunny Hat

■ pink and white construction paper, stapler, scissors

1. *Cut white construction paper, lengthwise, into 3" wide strips.*
2. *Staple two strips together to make a headband that fits a child's head snugly.*
3. *Cut out ears from pink construction paper.*
4. *Staple an ear on each side of the headband. Have the children do the bunny hop wearing their hats.*

Bunny Box

■ 1/2 pint milk cartons, rinsed and stapled shut; cotton balls; white craft glue; pink, orange, green and black construction paper; pink google eyes.

1. *Glue cotton balls on the milk carton until it's completely covered.*
2. *Cut out pink ears, black whiskers, an orange carrot and green carrot top from construction paper.*
3. *Glue on eyes, ears, whiskers, carrot and top.*

Easter Egg Hunt

Hide eggs filled with toys (see Favors) and have the children hunt for them. To make it easier for young children to find the eggs you've hidden, use stuffed bunnies and chicks as "pointers." This is a good way to make use of presents from Easters past. Older children will enjoy the game even more if you distribute written clues, such as "Underneath the maple tree, a treasure's hidden, look and see."

Fuzzy, Fuzzy Bunny Nose

Line the children up in two teams, as for a relay, and put Vaseline® on the tips of their noses. Place two piles of cotton balls at the other end of the room. Children must crawl to the pile and try to pick up one cotton ball with their noses (no hands!) then crawl back and let the next member try.

Baby Animal Game

Tape a picture of a baby animal to the back of each child and have them guess which animal it is by asking the other children such questions as "Does this animal swim?" or "Does this animal have fur?"

Easter Relay

Line the children up in two teams and give the first child in each line a basket. Place a bowl of jelly beans at the other end of the room. The children must waddle like a duck or hop like a bunny to the jelly bean stash, put one in the basket and hop or waddle back, then hand the basket to the next in line. Continue until all the jelly beans are gone.

Bunny Tail

Draw a bunny silhouette on a box and cut a hole where the tail should be. Place the box on a table at the children's level and have them use a straw to blow a ping-pong ball through the hole.

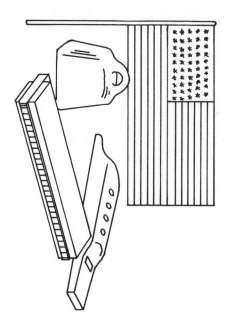

We the people of the 1400 block of East Avenue, in order to have a more perfect Fourth of July, invite you to a celebration in the street at 1 o'clock.

Independence Day Celebration

Flags fly and firecrackers explode. The Fourth of July offers us a wonderful opportunity to think about what freedom really means. How did Jefferson, Hancock, and Franklin feel as they signed the Declaration of Independence? What do phrases such as "all men are created equal" mean today? There's no better way to find out than to ask your guests to sign the Declaration of Independence themselves. Happy birthday to the U.S.A.! Happy birthday to us!

Declaration Invitation

■ white onionskin typing paper, fine-point black marker, black satin ribbon

1. *Write your own Declaration of Celebration, using words and phrases from the Declaration of Independence. For example, "When, in the course of human events, it becomes necessary for one people to celebrate Independence Day, the need for fun requires that they should gather at the Smith's house on July 4th at 12 o'clock." Or, use the Constitution as a model, "We the people of the 1400 block of East Avenue, in order to have a more perfect Fourth of July, invite you to a celebration in the street at 1 o'clock."*
2. *Write the invitation in long hand on onionskin paper.*
3. *Roll it like a scroll and tie it with black satin ribbon.*
4. *Hand deliver it to chosen lovers of liberty.*

Decorations

- For a neighborhood celebration, ask all the families to fly American flags in front of their houses.
- Tie red, white and blue balloons to fences, trees, and bushes.
- Use red, white and blue napkins, plates and tablecloths to decorate tables.
- Create a Fourth of July mural. (See Games and Activities)
- Make Independence Day Windsocks. (See Games and Activities)

Favors

Small flags to wave, bells to ring, kazoos and harmonicas for the parade, tricornered hats (see Games and Activities), sidewalk chalk, and traditional outdoor games such as jacks or marbles

Food

All-American Meal

Chicken on the Grill
Corn on the Cob
Watermelon Slices
Flag Salad
Brownies
Homemade Lemonade

Flag Salad

4 3-ounce packages red gelatin
2 8-ounce packages cream cheese, softened
milk
1-2 quarts strawberries
1 pint blueberries

Make gelatin in a 13" x 9" pan. Chill until set. Whip the softened cream cheese with just enough milk to make it spreading consistency. Frost the gelatin with the cream cheese. Wash and hull the strawberries, then arrange them to make stripes. Wash the blueberries and use them to make stars.

Games and Activities

Tricornered Hat

Make your own version of the hat Paul Revere and other Revolutionary War heroes wore.

Cut a piece of 9 x 12" black construction paper into three 12" strips. Place them end to end to form a triangle and staple the ends about 2" from the edge, to fit a child's head.

Fourth of July Mural

Cut a piece of butcher paper long enough to string across the street or from one end of your yard to the other and invite your friends to help decorate it with stars, stripes, fireworks and Fourth of July greetings.

Independence Day Windsocks

Make patriotic windsocks to hang from your porch or trees.

■ lightweight white posterboard, string, paper punch, red, white and blue crepe paper streamers, stapler, glue

1. Cut a 4 x 14" length of white posterboard.
2. Staple the ends together to form a ring.
3. Cut 30" red, white and blue crepe paper streamers.
4. Glue or staple them to the inside of the posterboard ring.
5. Thread a 24" piece of string through the holes and knot it at the top to make a hanger.

Fourth of July Parade

Line everyone up for an Independence Day Parade, some on bikes, some in wagons, and some marching with instruments such as kazoos, harmonicas and pots with spoons. Don't forget to include your pets and any parents willing to join in the fun. Wear your tricornered hats and sing patriotic songs, such as "Yankee Doodle Dandy."

Watermelon Eating Contest

This is a traditional American contest in which everyone is a winner. Give prizes to the person who can pile up the most seeds, the one who accumulates the most rinds, and the person who can spit seeds the farthest.

Three-Legged Race

Divide into teams made up of one adult and one child. Have the groups stand side by side and tie their inside legs together with rope or strips of fabric. The groups then race to the finish line.

Signing the Declaration of Independence

Buy or hand letter a copy of the Declaration of Independence and ask your guests to sign it. Discuss the meaning it had for the original signers and the meaning it has today.

Balloon Launch

Buy enough red, white and blue helium-filled balloons and stamped postcards for each of your guests. Guests fill out cards with their home addresses on one side and Fourth of July greetings on the other. They should add postscripts asking the finders of the balloons to drop the cards in the mail. Then use a paper punch to make holes in the cards and tie them to the balloon strings. Let all the balloons free at the same time.

Halloween Party

Whoooo's having a party? You are! Light the jack-o-lanterns, scare up some snacks and give your friends another excuse to wear their costumes. Halloween's too much fun to be over in one day.

Jack-O'-Lantern Invitation

■ orange balloons, indelible black fine-point marker, envelopes

1. *Blow* up a balloon and hold it by the neck, without tying it, while you draw a jack-o'-lantern face on one side and write the party information on the other side.
2. *Deflate* the balloon and mail it.

Decorations

• Seat a scarecrow, made of old clothes stuffed with newspaper, by your front door to welcome guests. Give him a floppy hat to wear on his brown bag head.

• Drape orange and black paper chains around the room.

• Cut out black construction paper bats and suspend them from the ceiling with black thread.

• Create spooky lighting by using colored light bulbs.

• For an evening party, carve the letters P-A-R-T-Y on five pumpkins. Light a candle in each and set them on your walkway or porch.

• Carve a face on two sides of a hollowed pumpkin to create a two-faced jack-o'-lantern. Place a glass of hot water inside the pumpkin and float a chunk of dry ice in the water. Spooky fog will float out of the eyes, nose and mouth.

• Make spider place cards.

■ black pompons, 10-12" black pipe cleaners, blank index cards, glue

1. *Cut* two pipe cleaners in half.
2. *Wind* those four pieces around each other at the center and *twist* them to make eight squiggly legs.
3. *Glue* a black pompon on top for the spider's body.
4. *Cut* a small strip from an index card and *write* the child's name on it.
5. *Glue* the card to one of the spider's legs.

• Decorate a holiday tree with lollipop ghost favors.

Whoooo's having a party?

Jacob

Please come.
Wear costumes.

Saturday
Oct. 24
1 - 3

Beth

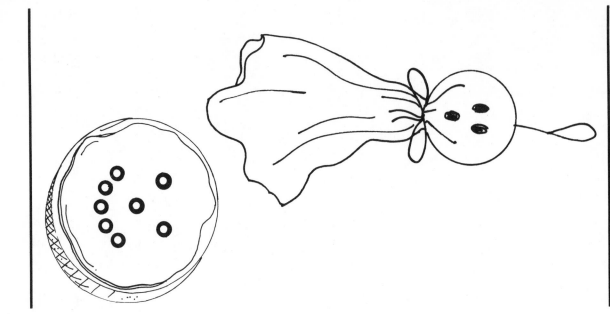

■ white cheesecloth, white facial tissue, Tootsie Roll Pops® or other ball-shaped lollipops, black thread, black fine-point marker.

1. *Cut a 12 x 12" double layer of cheesecloth.*
2. *Cover the lollipop first with a double layer of facial tissue, then with a square of cheesecloth.*
3. *Tie black thread around the base of the lollipop to secure the cheesecloth, leaving an extra loop of thread to hang the ghost.*
4. *Draw the ghost's face with black marker.*

Favors

Polaroid® picture of each child in costume, Halloween stickers, plastic spider rings, apples, lollipop ghosts, sandwich bags filled with popcorn, balls of orange play dough in plastic bags tied with green yarn

1 cup flour
1/2 cup salt
2 tablespoons oil
2 teaspoons cream of tartar

1 cup water
few drops red and yellow food
  coloring

Mix all ingredients in a pot. Cook, stirring, over medium heat until thick. Knead while warm. Store in airtight plastic bags.

Food

Frightfully Good Lunch

Jack-O'Lantern Sandwiches
Carrot and Raisin Salad
Toasted Pumpkin Seeds
Peanut Butter Worms
Cider or Milk

Jack-O'Lantern Sandwiches

Cut bread in circles. Top with circular yellow cheese slices. Place under broiler until cheese melts. Children can arrange sliced black olives or pieces of crumbled bacon to make a jack-o'-lantern face.

Carrot and Raisin Salad

2 cups grated carrot
1/2 cup raisins
small can crushed pineapple
foil muffin liners

Mix all ingredients and moisten with mayonnaise if desired. Serve in muffin liners. Serves 6 to 8.

Toasted Pumpkin Seeds

Separate the seeds from the pulp and wash them. Dry on paper towels overnight. Spread the seeds on a cookie sheet and dot with oil or margarine. Sprinkle with salt or parmesan cheese. Bake at 350 degrees for 20 minutes.

Peanut Butter Worms

1 cup peanut butter
1/2 cup honey
1 1/2 cups nonfat dry milk solids
1/2 cup confectioners' sugar
raisins and peanuts

Mix peanut butter and honey in a medium bowl. Stir in nonfat dry milk solids and confectioners' sugar until blended. Roll dough balls between your hands to make fat "worms." Use raisins or peanuts to make eyes. Chill at least 30 minutes to set before serving. Makes 2 dozen.

Games and Activities

Pumpkin Place Mats

Children can make their own Halloween place mats using 12 x 18" sheets of orange construction paper cut into pumpkin shapes. Let the children decorate with fluorescent crayons or markers or glue on green and black shapes cut from construction paper to create facial features.

Costume Parade

Have the children parade while you play scary music. Take Polaroid® snapshots of each guest. Award ribbons, made with orange construction paper, black crepe paper and Halloween stickers, to each participant.

Halloween Ride

Divide the children into two teams. The first child on each team wears a witch's hat and rides a broom to a point and back, then passes the broom and hat to the next child. For more of a challenge, set up an obstacle course for the broom riders.

Witch's Brew

Give each child a list of items to find and deposit in a large cauldron or pot. The lists can include items such as three yellow leaves, a round stone, a dead flower, an acorn, etc. When all the items are found and deposited, make a production of stirring the brew while the children chant, "Bubble, bubble. Stir it double. Witch's brew is no trouble." Then reach to the bottom of the pot and pull out a favor for each child.

Pumpkin Toss

Toss bean bags, crumpled paper or bags filled with popcorn into a large plastic pumpkin.

Evil Spell

Pretend that an evil witch has cast a spell and in order to break it the children must recite this poem: "Hair of bat, wicked brew. Tell us now what (child's name) must do." Then the child chooses a "trick" written on a slip of paper from a witch's hat or plastic pumpkin. The tricks should have a Halloween flavor: walk like a spider, cackle like a witch, etc.

Spooky Sound Effects

Choose a Halloween book that mentions lots of eerie noises. *That Terrible Halloween Night* by James Stevenson is a good choice because it's noisy, scary and funny, too. Then ask the children to imitate creaking doors, shrieking ghosts, and other spooky sounds while you tape their performance. Play back the tape as you read the story.

Bobbing For Apples

Float apples in a washtub, children's swimming pool or dishpan, and have the children put their hands behind their backs and try to pick them up with their teeth.

Halloween Huff and Puff

Place a jack-o'-lantern on a table at the children's level with a candle inside. Blindfold the children, one at a time, their hands behind their backs, twirling them around as they start toward the pumpkin. The object is to blow out the candle. An adult must watch to be sure the children don't accidentally knock the pumpkin off the table.

Chanukah Party

Chanukah, the Festival of Lights, celebrates the victory of Judah Maccabee, who fought to reclaim the Temple of Jerusalem from the Syrians. When the battle was over, they could find only a small amount of the oil — a day's worth — needed to consecrate the temple, but that oil miraculously burned for eight days while a runner was sent for more. Because of this, the menorah has eight candles, with an extra candle, called the shammash, used to light one candle each day until all are burning.

Menorah Invitation

■ 9 x 12" white construction paper, glitter writer, blue marker, scissors

1. *Cut* a 9 x 12" piece of white construction paper in half to make two 9 x 6" pieces.
2. *Fold* one piece in half to make a 4 1/2 x 6" card.
3. *Draw* a menorah and candles with blue marker on the front of the card.
4. *Use* glitter writer to make a flame over the same number of candles that you will light on the day of your party. For example, if the party will be on the fourth day of Chanukah, "light" four candles.
5. *Write* the invitation inside the card.

Decorations

Draw paper dreidels and Stars of David, and hang them with blue and white crepe paper streamers. Have a real menorah, ready to light, as the centerpiece.

Favors

Dreidels (see Games and Activities), small flashlights or pen lights, Chanukah gelt (chocolate coins wrapped in gold foil), and stencils or stickers with symbols of Chanukah such as the hammer, the lion and the menorah

Food

Chanukah Lunch
Potato Latkes with Apple Sauce or Sour Cream
Candle Salad
Chanukah Cookies
Milk

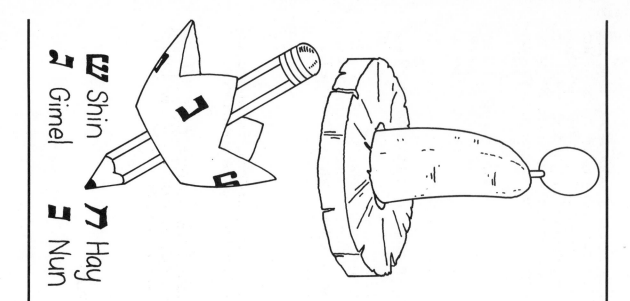

ש Shin   ה Hay

ג Gimel   נ Nun

Potato Latkes

2 cups grated potatoes
3 eggs
1 1/2 tablespoons matzo meal or flour
salt and pepper to taste
oil

Grate the potatoes and pour off the liquid. Beat the eggs and combine with remaining ingredients. Make into patties and fry in very hot oil. Serve with applesauce or sour cream.

Candle Salad

6 canned pineapple rings
3 bananas
6 red grapes
6 toothpicks

Cut a banana in half and stand it in a pineapple ring on a salad plate. Use a toothpick to anchor a grape on top for a flame. Makes 6.

Chanukah Cookies

Use candle, lion, or dreidel-shaped cookie cutters to cut Chanukah cookies from your favorite butter or sugar cookie recipe.

Games and Activities

Egg Carton Dreidel
■ Styrofoam® or cardboard egg carton, pencils, pen

1. Cut one cup from the bottom of the egg carton.
2. Cut out triangular shapes, starting at the top to make four pointed petals.
3. Push a sharp pencil halfway through the cup.
4. Write the Hebrew letters Shin, Hay, Gimel, and Nun, one on each side, using the pen. The letters stand for the Hebrew words meaning, "A Great Miracle Happened Here."

Dreidel Game

To play dreidel, give everyone 10 or 15 pennies or raisins. Each player puts one in the pot, and one player spins the dreidel. If the letter that comes up is Nun, he gets nothing; if it's Gimel, he gets the whole pot; if it's Hay, he gets half; and if it's Shin, he must add one to the pot. Each time the pot empties, all the players must add one to the pot.

Spinning Tops

Have the children practice spinning the tops before you begin. Then have them pretend their bodies are spinning tops as they sing, "We are little spinning tops, going round and round. Now we're getting slower, and now we're on the ground," with appropriate pantomime.

Light the Menorah

Give everyone a chance to light one of the candles on the menorah, then stand around the table singing songs such as "Rock of Ages" (Maoz Tzur) and "My Dreidel".

My Dreidel

I have a little dreidel,
I made it out of clay;
When it's dry and ready,
Then dreidel I will play.
Dreidel, dreidel, dreidel,
I made it out of clay.
Dreidel, dreidel, dreidel
Now dreidel I will play.

Treasure Hunt

Hide the Chanukah gelt, then write clues that will lead to the treasure and hide the clues, too. The first clue is given to each player at the start. If the child solves the first clue, it will lead to the second, which will lead to the third, and so on.

Christmas Party

Children love Christmas. Who doesn't? Since your house is already decked out in Christmas finery, why not invite some friends over to share this special holiday?

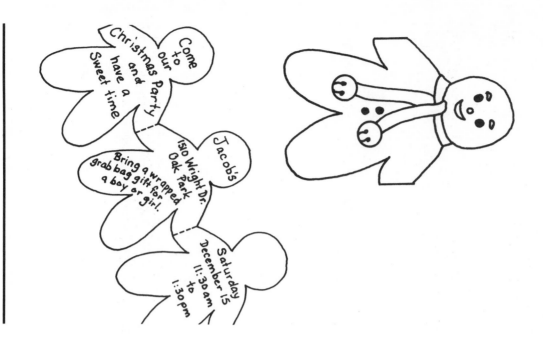

Invitation   (Makes 6)

■ Six 9 x 12" sheets of brown construction paper, 2 yards red satin or curling ribbon. Twelve 1/2" jingle bells, small colorful candies, scissors, glue

1. *Fold* a sheet of contruction paper in thirds lengthwise and draw a gingerbread man (about 6" long), making sure that the arms extend all the way to the folds.

2. *Cut* all three layers, as you would for paper dolls, leaving the arms attached.

3. *Write* a message inside, then refold and glue candy on top to make the face and buttons.

4. When dry, *tie* a red ribbon "scarf" around the neck. *Thread* a jingle bell on each end of the scarf and tie a knot to secure it.

Decorations

- If you've already decorated for Christmas, you won't need much more. To carry out the theme of the invitation, bake gingerbread men and hang them on the wreath on your door or your tree.

- Make chains of gingerbread men from construction paper, or from brown wrapping paper, as you did for the invitations, and tie them together with red ribbon to make a garland for your tree. Or hang gingerbread men garlands from the ceiling, as you would crepe paper streamers.

- Set the table with a red tablecloth and green plates.

- For place cards, cut out gingerbread men from brown construction paper, write guests' names on the front, and glue them to small white paper cups. Fill the cups with nuts and raisins.

- Use a graham cracker "gingerbread" house for the centerpiece.

Graham Cracker "Gingerbread" House

■ 1 box graham crackers, one-gallon wax paper milk carton or similar size box, gum drops, red licorice, candy canes, peppermint pinwheels, lollipops, and other assorted candies

Measure and cut down the box or milk carton to form a house that matches the illustration. Use a scissors and perhaps a knife to do this, then tape the edges with masking tape.

Frosting

2 egg whites
3 1/2 cups confectioners sugar (sifted)
1/2 teaspoon cream of tartar

Beat egg whites until stiff but not dry. Gradually add sifted confectioners sugar and cream of tartar. Beat until stiff. Cover with a damp cloth to keep from drying out. Using the frosting as you would glue, attach a row of double graham crackers around the base of the box, then use double graham crackers to make a roof that hangs over the base as a real roof would. The triangular peaks at either end should be spread with icing and filled with candies or marshmallows. Use red licorice sticks or candy canes at each corner. Decorate the rest of the house with assorted candies.

Favors

Snow shakers (see Games and Activities), Christmas books, reindeer candy canes (see Games and Activities), Christmas stickers, miniature nativity sets, ornaments, or almost anything wrapped as a gift.

Food

Merry Christmas Lunch
Gingerbread Men Sandwiches
Gelatin Christmas Trees
Red Grapes
Hot Chocolate

Gingerbread Men Sandwiches
Using a cookie cutter, cut gingerbread men out of whole wheat bread. Fill sandwiches with peanut butter and jelly and decorate with raisins for face and buttons. A dab of peanut butter on the raisins will keep them in place.

Gelatin Christmas Trees
Make a large box of lime gelatin in a jelly roll pan. When firm, cut Christmas trees out of gelatin using an oiled cookie cutter. Slide a spatula under the cookie cutter in order to transfer the gelatin to each plate.

Hot Chocolate
Serve with miniature marshmallows and candy cane stir sticks.

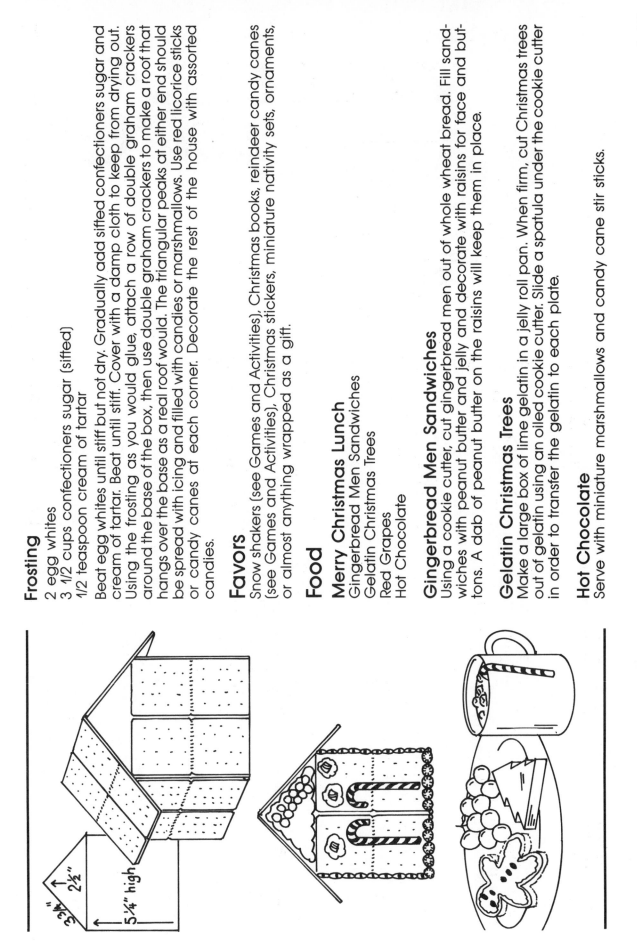

Games and Activities

Snow Shakers

■ baby food jars, glitter, felt, small Christmas figurines, waterproof glue, ribbon

1. *Glue* figurines to the inside of the lid.
2. When dry, place 2 teaspoons glitter in the jar and *fill* with water.
3. *Apply* glue to the inside threads of the lid and screw the lid on.
4. *Glue* a circle of felt to the lid and *tie* a ribbon around the jar's neck.

Reindeer Hunt

Make reindeer by gluing google eyes and red pompon noses on wrapped candy canes, then winding red or green pipe cleaners around the top to make antlers. Hide them around the house, and send the children to find them. You can also play this game with one child as It and the others helping to find a hidden reindeer, by shouting "warmer" or "colder" as the child moves toward or away from the candy cane. Let each guest have a turn.

Jingle Bell Freeze

Thread jingle bells on pipe cleaners and attach one to each child's leg. Then have the children sing and dance along with a recording of "Jingle Bells" or "Jingle Bell Rock." Shout "freeze" and stop the music occasionally. If anyone's bells jingle, you will know they've moved.

Christmas Trivia Contest

Make up a list of Christmas questions appropriate to the age of your guests, such as "How did the three wise men find the stable where Jesus was born?" and "Name one of Santa's reindeer." To reduce competitiveness, let everyone shout out the answers, and award stickers to all at the end.

Reindeer Tag

A child who is It tries to tag the others, who must put their hands up like antlers once they've been tagged. The last child turned into a reindeer becomes It.

Musical Presents

Ask guests to bring a wrapped grab bag gift, suitable for a girl or boy. They will be just as delighted if you ask them to wrap up a used toy, but if you ask for new toys, be sure to set a limit on what they're to spend. When it's time to distribute the gifts, play Christmas music and have the children sit in a circle and pass all of the gifts in the same direction. When the music stops, they each unwrap the present they're holding. As an alternative, consider asking the children to bring a wrapped gift to be given to a worthy cause.

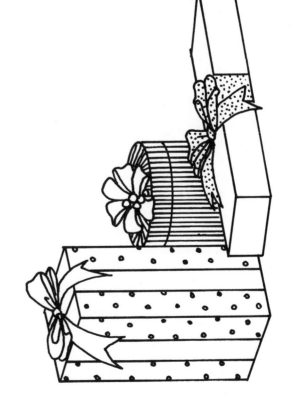

Celebrate the Seasons

We teach our children about the life-giving, spirit-lifting power of nature by sharing it with them. In celebrating the seasons, we remind ourselves to pay attention to and savor the natural world, something which the pace of our lives all too often allows us to forget.

Take time to wander on a beach together, stand in the filtered light of a forest or tromp through a snowy field. When you've had enough of the first robin, first crocus, first bush to leaf out, first earthworm, and so on. Record which family member spotted each first, where and when.

Joy in nature is one of the few gifts you can give your child that won't break or wear out. By encouraging our children to develop a respect for and love of nature, we're helping them to develop attitudes that are needed to sustain the planet and the human race.

Spring

- Spring is a time for returns and new beginnings. Make a chart for your refrigerator or bulletin board with spaces for the first robin, first crocus, first bush to leaf out, first earthworm, and so on. Record which family member spotted each first, where and when.

- Cut branches from a forsythia bush, bring them indoors and put them in water. The warmth will make them burst into bloom. You can also force tulips or hyacinths by planting bulbs indoors in a container full of potting soil. Keep the soil moist.

- Mark the first day of spring by bringing bunches of daffodils to special people in your lives. Save a bunch to adorn your own table and serve a spring brunch of Eggs Benedict, asparagus tips and fresh strawberries.

- Work together to start seeds for your vegetable garden or flower garden. Plant seeds indoors in starting cups, flats or Styrofoam® cups. Water and watch the plants every day for a month or so, then transplant to an outdoor garden when the weather is right. As you and your child work, you can talk about the things seeds need to grow, and why spring is the time when planting is done.

ITEMS	SEEN BY	DATE	WHERE SEEN			
FIRST ROBIN						
FIRST FLOWER						
FIRST BUSH WITH LEAVES						
FIRST WORM						

SPRING

SEED DETECTIVE

- Present your children with official "Seed Detective" badges made of cardboard covered with foil. Tape a safety pin to the back and write "Seed Detective" on the front with a ball point pen. Tell them they're on special assignment to search for and collect all the seeds served in food over the next few days. Serve foods such as oranges, apples, grapes, melons, tomatoes, cucumbers, pomegranates, avocados, beans and rice. A box lid will make a good place to display the growing collection. You might also want to plant your seeds to see what sprouts. Collect seeds outdoors from trees, bushes and dandelions to add to your collection.

- Serve a seed lunch. Make your own peanut butter by shelling roasted peanuts, removing the skins and placing the peanuts in a blender jar with 1 1/2 tablespoons corn oil. Blend on high, then spread peanut butter on bread, apple slices or pieces of celery. Cook corn or peas to go with your peanut butter, and point out that they are also seeds. You can open a package of corn or bean seeds to compare the ones you eat and the ones you plant. Use the remaining seeds to design a spring greeting card or sign for your front door. Serve toasted sunflower seeds, and spoon strawberries or raspberries over ice cream for dessert. Find the seeds.

- Invite friends or neighbors to a celebration of spring and ask your guests to bring something from winter that they'd like to give away. Make a "Welcome Spring" banner for the front of your house, and decorate it with fresh flowers. Begin the celebration with a reading of E.E. Cummings' poems to spring.

- Take wildflower walks, and identify what you see with a field guide. Random House publishes a series of small Audubon Society Beginner Guides, including one on wildflowers. Don't pick the flowers. Take photographs or draw pictures. A magnifying glass helps. Keep a book of everything your family has seen on these outings, including dates and places.

- Birds that have wintered in other parts of the country should begin arriving in early March. Even if you live in an urban area, there are many species you can spot passing through your neighborhood during the spring migration. Use your ears as well as eyes and you'll learn to identify birds by their songs. On weekends, take bird walks and keep a running record of the birds you see over the years. Be sure to bring field glasses.

- Go fly a kite. Cut a bird shape from a double layer of tissue paper and glue the two matching pieces together around the edges. Attach a string at the head and run in the wind.

- Arbor Day is a good time to plant a new tree, contribute to an organization that will plant one for you, or do something nice for a tree that lives in your backyard. It's also a good day to take a hike through a forest or just celebrate with the trees in your neighborhood. Climb one. How far can you see? Swing on one. Wrap your arms around its trunk. Then sit in its shade, take a deep breath of the oxygen it helps create and look for birds or squirrels in the branches. Make bark rubbings by placing a white sheet of paper against the trunk and rubbing with a crayon. The bark pattern will appear on the paper. Serve a lunch made from things that grow on trees, and give thanks for all the gifts we get from them.

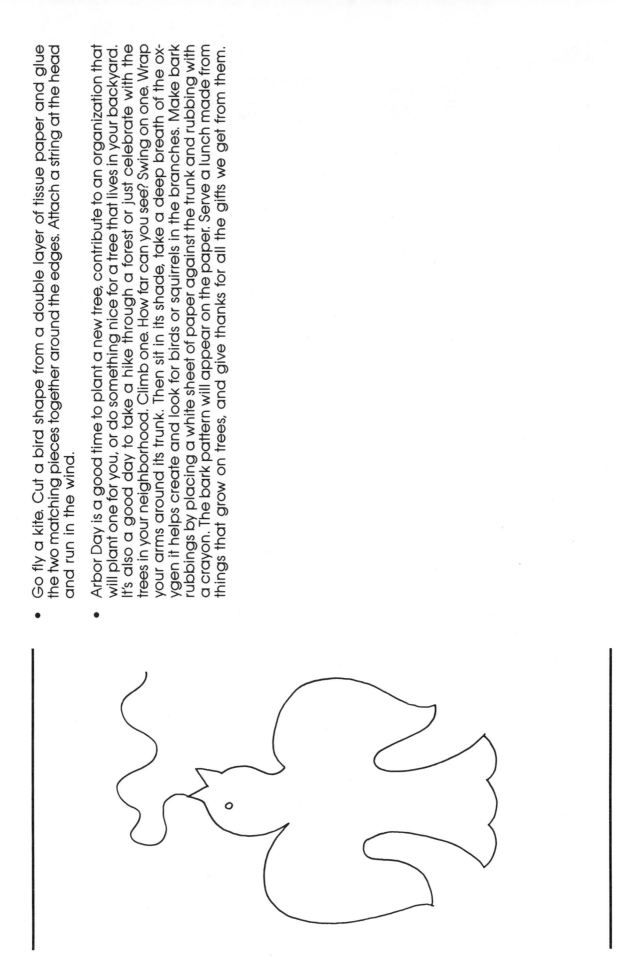

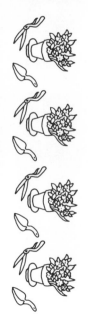

Summer

- The summer solstice occurs on June 21 in the Northern Hemisphere. It is the time when the sun appears highest in the sky and the time when the days are longest. Europeans light fires on hilltops to warm the earth and scare away witches on Midsummer Eve, the night before the solstice. Stay up late reading books together. If you have older children, you may want to borrow a tape of Shakespeare's *Midsummer Night's Dream* from the library. When it gets dark, catch fireflies and put them in a glass jar with some grass and weeds to serve as your "bonfire." Then take a star walk together and look for constellations.

- An inexpensive butterfly net can provide children with hours and hours of fun. Instead of mounting and collecting butterflies, observe their markings, sketch and color them, then set them free. Cut out your paper butterflies, attach thread and run in the wind, watching them flutter behind you. Or use your butterflies to make a mobile.

- June and July are berry months. You may find raspberries, strawberries or blueberries at U-pick farms in your area, or you may be lucky enough to live in a place where there are edible berries growing wild. Call the food section of your newspaper or your local tourist office for information about U-pick farms. Be sure to call the farms in advance since the growing seasons are short, and ask if you should bring your own containers. Eat the berries fresh. They won't need sugar if you pick them ripe. Give some away to friends and neighbors. Berries which are difficult to transport, like raspberries, are much cheaper when you pick them yourself than they are in stores. Friends will consider them a great delicacy. If you have any left over, freeze some, bake pies or make jam.

- Summer is a good time to have a backyard campout. Set up a tent, pack a picnic dinner and snacks, and be sure to bring along a canteen and flashlights. You can use the flashlights to play flashlight tag (it touches you with the beam from his or her light), to make shadow pictures on the walls of your tent, and to substitute for a campfire when you sit around spinning yarns. Tell ghost stories or use your own names to make up an adventure story, with each storyteller picking up where the previous narrator leaves off. Before you go to sleep, turn off the flashlight and listen for night sounds. Can you hear frogs? An owl? A raccoon looking for a meal?

- Take as many weekend excursions as you can this summer. They'll be more fun if you plan them around a theme. Spend a day at a nature preserve looking for animal homes. Can you find tent caterpillars? Bird or squirrel nests? Snake or animal holes? Spider webs? Another week, go on a bug hunt, equipped with magnifying glasses. Pond life makes another interesting theme. Look for tadpoles, frogs, turtles, fish, water bugs and plant life. *Nature With Children of All Ages* is a resource book that is loaded with outdoor activities. It's written by Edith A. Sisson of the Massachusetts Audubon Society and was published by Prentice-Hall in 1982.

- The beach is another wonderful place to observe nature. Collect rocks or pebbles, build sand castles, skip stones, look for shells, chase the waves and let the waves chase you.

- Some foods remind us of certain seasons of the year because they're at their best then. The smell of apple pie baking, the flavor of fresh strawberry shortcake or the aroma of pot roast and carrots simmering in a warm kitchen can evoke many memories. Make a tradition of celebrating the arrival of seasonal foods with a special meal. If you have a garden, you can harvest the food together. Otherwise, try to visit a farm stand or farmers' market. Celebrate the first garden salad, the first homemade spaghetti sauce, the first zucchini bread and the first roast corn.

- On the hottest day of the summer, squeeze lemons and make your own lemonade or make popsicles or ice cream from scratch.

- Take a barefoot walk and explore the grass, the sidewalk, the dirt, a smooth board. Which is hottest? Which is softest? Which is hardest?

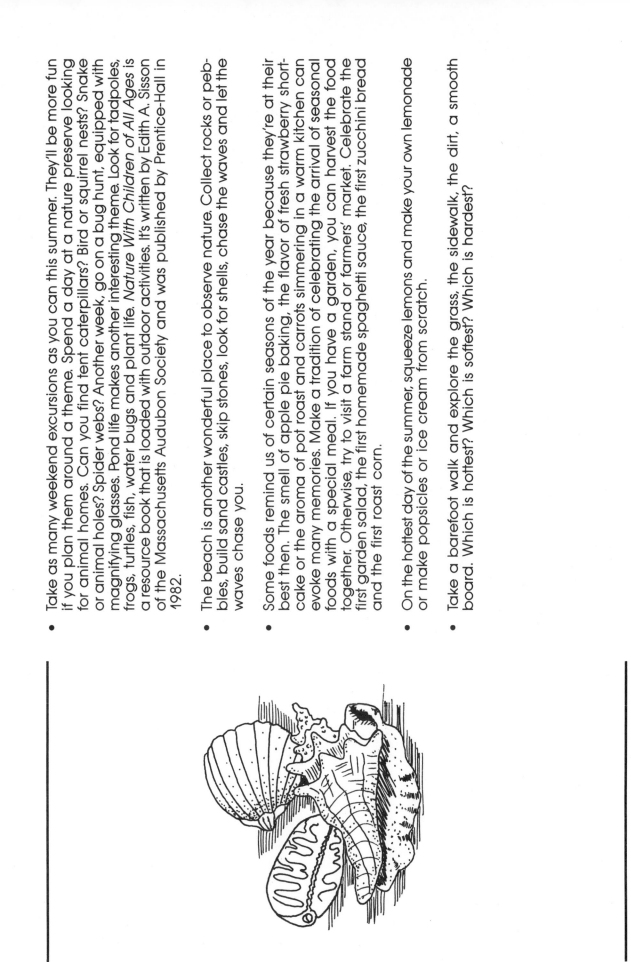

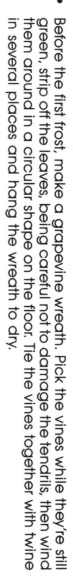

Autumn

- Before the first frost, make a grapevine wreath. Pick the vines while they're still green, strip off the leaves, being careful not to damage the tendrils, then wind them around in a circular shape and hang the wreath to dry. Tie the vines together with twine in several places and hang the wreath to dry.

- Find an orchard where you can pick your own apples, and pick an extra bushel to give to a soup kitchen or food pantry. If you're lucky, you may get a ride on a hay wagon thrown in for free. When you get home, celebrate your harvest by serving mugs of hot cider with cinnamon stir sticks and powdered sugar donuts or gingerbread cookies. Later, make applesauce.

- Fall is hiking, biking and horseback riding weather. Choose a bright, crisp autumn morning when the color is at its peak and head for the woods. Stand under a yellow maple and enjoy the golden world.

- Leaf raking is a great family activity, especially if you get to jump in a pile of leaves when you're done. Be sure to get scaled-down rakes so even the youngest can help.

- Make a fall candle holder. Collect pine cones, seeds and nuts, then glue them on a cardboard ring and coat with polyurethane or a clear plastic spray. Stand a tall candle in the center when it's dry.

- As you stand at the threshold of winter, show the world you still believe in spring. Collect fallen seeds from flowers, plants, and trees. Let everyone in the family browse through gardening catalogues, choose some bulbs and help plant them when they arrive. You might also want to choose and plant bulbs as a surprise for a friend.

- Celebrate the harvest with a meal planned around a large pot of vegetable soup. Pick the ingredients from your garden, or buy them at a farm stand. While you and your children are cleaning and cutting the vegetables, discover the differences in size, shape, color and texture. Save a few vegetables to polish and put in a basket as a centerpiece. During the meal, talk about the ingredients necessary for a successful harvest: seeds, sun, rain and people to pull the weeds, plow the soil and bring the food to market. Before bed, read Marcia Brown's Stone Soup.

- Decorate your home with leaf rubbings. Tape leaves that are not yet brittle to pieces of heavy paper or cardboard, place typing paper over the leaves and rub with the side of an unwrapped crayon. Mount the rubbings on construction paper and hang them around the house.

- Make a fall table runner by cutting a 12"-wide strip of butcher paper, as long as your table, and decorating it with apple prints. Cut an apple in half, dip it in red paint and press it on the paper. Use green marker to make stems.

- On one of your walks, look for weeds and grasses to make an arrangement for your door or a vase. To dry flowers, pick them on a warm day when there is no moisture on the plant. Remove excess leaves, then tie the flowers in bunches and hang them upside down in a warm, dry place for about two weeks. Never pick wildflowers or remove any plants from parks or public lands.

Winter

- The winter solstice occurs on December 21. It is the shortest day of the year, the day when the sun is at its lowest point in the sky. In earlier times, people tried to encourage the sun in its battle against darkness by lighting fires at the time of the winter solstice. Their efforts were always rewarded. The earth warmed, the days began to get longer and light triumphed over darkness, as it does today and as it has for centuries. Each civilization has its own way of celebrating light. The Romans saw the solstice as a time to look ahead to spring. Their Saturnalia festival, which honored the god of sowing grain, was a raucous week-long feast. Jews celebrate Chanukah, the Festival of Lights, and Christians celebrate the birth of Christ, the Light of the World. On the evening of the winter solstice, light a candle before dinner and give thanks for the wonderful round of seasons. Remember that, although there are cold days ahead, each day will get a little longer and spring will return.

- Don't let winter keep you indoors. Go cross-country skiing or take a hike in the still winter woods. Watch a sunset and note how different winter's icy purples and blues are from the flame of a summer sunset. Look for footprints in the snow. Who else is venturing out in the cold?

- Read *The Winter Picnic* by Robert Welber, bundle up and have hot mugs of soup at the picnic table.

- Many artists think that trees are at their loveliest in winter because you can see their intricate skeletons. Pick a special tree in your neighborhood to photograph or paint. Then capture the same tree in the spring, the summer and the fall. Hang the pictures side by side in your home.

- On the day of the first good snow, invite some friends to a "Let it Snow" party. Supply sticks, rocks, carrots, lettuce leaves and old hats for building snowpeople. Find a hilly spot and bring your sleds. Go ice skating. Lie on your back and make snow angels. Or play Fox and Geese. Make a circle with spokes in the snow by packing it down with your feet. One person is chosen to be the fox and chases the geese around the circle and spokes until he tags someone who then becomes the fox. When you're cold and tired, come inside for hot chocolate and snowball cookies made by frosting large sugar cookies and sprinkling them with coconut.

- Fondue in front of the fireplace is an ideal way to entertain friends or family on winter evenings. If you don't have a fireplace, choose a cozy spot where you can gather on pillows around a small table. Dip chunks of beef sirloin, chicken breast, fresh mushrooms or shrimp in a fondue pot filled with oil and serve with barbeque sauce, hollandaise sauce, horseradish sauce or other dips. A large fresh green salad and crusty French bread will complete the meal. Anyone whose meat falls from a fork into the oil must make a wish, reveal a dream, sing a song or recite a poem.

- The cold weather and long nights of winter offer a good excuse to spend more time together as a family. Choose one night each week when you can all be at home. Turn off the television, make a big bowl of popcorn and spend your winter's eve playing board games, reading out loud, telling stories, doing a jigsaw puzzle together or singing songs.

- When you're longing for spring, sprout alfalfa seeds on your window sill. To make a sprouter, remove the center of a mason jar lid and replace it with a round piece of plastic or wire mesh. Soak the seeds overnight in the jar, then pour off the water and rinse them daily until they're ready to eat.

- Work on a cloth or paper banner which proclaims "It's Spring!!" Count the days until you can hang it up.

Celebrate Life

Create-an-Occasion Parties

A spur-of-the-moment party that doesn't focus on any particular event or person can provide your family and a few friends with lots of happiness and some wonderful memories. Cure a case of summer vacation blahs or wintertime cabin fever by surprising your family with a party to celebrate the simple joy of being a family.

Jungle Breakfast

Before the family wakes up some warm morning, sneak outside and hide breakfast in the trees and bushes. Individual boxes of cereal, hard-boiled eggs, oranges, bananas, muffins in plastic sandwich bags and juice boxes are easy to hide. Leave a message on the kitchen table directing the family to the hunt.

While everyone rushes out to search for breakfast, bring milk, plates, cups, and flatware to an outdoor picnic table. At the end of breakfast, use verbal clues to direct everyone in a new search for a well hidden coconut — real jungle fruit. End the morning celebration by opening the coconut and sharing the delicious meat. To open a coconut you need a hammer and a screwdriver. Pound a hole in each of the three "eyes" of the coconut, drain the coconut milk into an empty container, split open the shell and enjoy the coconut. Grate any uneaten coconut and refrigerate. Use in salads, cookies or trail mix.

Doughnut Breakfast Party

The day before the party, make doughnut invitations and give them to family members or two or three friends. On a 6 x 6" piece of brown construction paper, glue a white paper doughnut. Write the party information around the doughnut. "Doughnut you want to come to a Doughnut Breakfast Party? Saturday at 9 a.m." Serve fresh fruit, sausage links, milk and, of course, doughnuts. Play a few doughnut games after breakfast. For *Dangling Doughnuts*, hang doughnuts on a string and eat with hands behind the back. Play *Penny Pitch* by placing three doughnuts on a piece of cardboard. Stand six feet away and pitch pennies into the doughnut holes. Give the doughnuts to the birds after the party, if they're not too sugary. Put a doughnut into a plastic bag, have everyone sit in a circle and play *Hot Doughnut* (play like Hot Potato).

"Green Eggs and Ham" Breakfast

Invite several friends to come for a special breakfast. Borrow *Green Eggs and Ham* by Dr. Seuss from the library for an adult to read while having a breakfast of green eggs and ham.

IT'S JUNGLE BREAKFAST DAY!

All eaters must **find and pick** breakfast from the trees and bushes in our "jungle yard."

Meet at the picnic table when you have **gathered** your bounty.

9A.M.
DOUGHNUT YOU WANT TO COME TO A DOUGHNUT BREAKFAST PARTY DOUGHNUT. SAT.

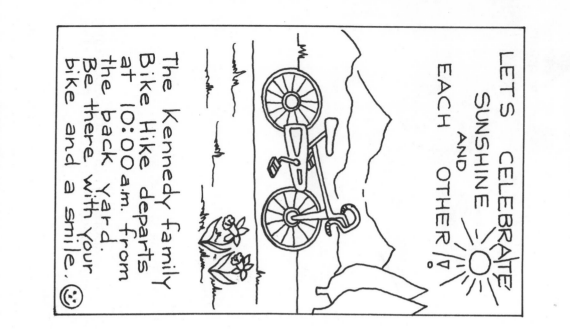

LET'S CELEBRATE SUNSHINE AND EACH OTHER!

The Kennedy family Bike Hike departs at 10:00 a.m. from the back Yard. Be there with Your bike and a smile. ☺

Green Eggs and Ham

4 eggs
1/4 cup milk
2 tablespoons finely chopped spinach
1 tablespoon butter or margarine
1/4 cup diced, cooked ham

1. *Melt the butter or margarine in a frying pan over medium heat.*
2. *Mix together the eggs, milk, spinach and ham.*
3. *Pour into the frying pan and cook until done. Serves 4.*

Serve with warm rolls or toast, juice and milk.

Bike Hike Lunch

At breakfast on a sunny day, present each family member with a special invitation for a family bike hike.

Pack a backpack with sandwiches, fresh fruit, trail mix, favorite cookies and individual cans or boxes of chilled juice. The age of the children will determine the length of the ride. A nearby park for play and lunch will be fun for young children. If your children are older choose a special spot at a greater distance. To add to the enjoyment, write step-by-step directions, detailing turns and distances while keeping the destination a mystery. Give the directions to the children and have them lead the way. If you wish, you can provide each person with several 10-foot long crepe paper streamers and some tape with the invitations. Tell them to decorate their bikes before the hike.

Rainy Day Picnic

Invite your children to a picnic on a rainy day. Spread a large blanket on the floor in the dining room or family room. Pack lunch in a picnic basket and feast on the floor. During lunch create imaginary settings for your party, with each person describing his or her ideal picnic spot. Spark imaginations by writing picnic sites on slips of paper that are drawn out of a bag. The beach, a mountain top, an apple orchard, a cave in the woods, a park, or the zoo are all inspiring locations. After lunch, cover the kitchen table with newspapers and enjoy "Rock Art." Collect 4- to 6-inch smooth rocks ahead of time and tuck them away. Provide the rocks, small paint brushes, jars of tempera paint and spray polyurethane to protect the finished products. The painted rocks make wonderful paperweights or decorations for a shelf. A piece of felt glued to the bottom renders them scratch-proof.

Treasure Hunt Lunch

Wrap sandwiches, carrot sticks, fresh fruit, raisins, cookies and juice boxes or small juice cans in aluminum foil. Hide everything around the yard and tell the children to search for their lunch. For more fun, give the children a treasure map to follow. In cold weather, have an indoor hunt.

Bubble Party

Invite a few friends for an afternoon of bubbly adventures. For favors, buy plastic bottles of bubbles, sugarless bubble gum and bubble pipes. Serve Bubble Snack:

Bubble Puffs,
Gum Ball Machine Treat
Bubbly Cooler.

Bubble Puffs

One package Party Rolls (20 in a package)
One jar Old English® cheese
1/4 pound butter or margarine

1. *Split* the rolls in half.
2. *Cream* butter and cheese until smooth.
3. *Spread* cut sides of rolls with cheese mixture.
4. *Place* on baking sheets and bake at 425 degrees for 10 minutes or until lightly browned and bubbly.

Gum Ball Machine Treat

Invert a 3 1/2-ounce clear plastic cup over green, purple and red grapes.

Bubbly Cooler

Mix orange juice concentrate with three cans of sparkling water for a bubbly drink. Freeze seedless grapes or strawberries in ice cubes and float one in each glass.

Bubble Games

Make a bubble solution by mixing 2/3 cup of liquid dishwashing detergent with one gallon of water in a bucket. Add 1 tablespoon of glycerine. Aging the solution for five days makes it work better.

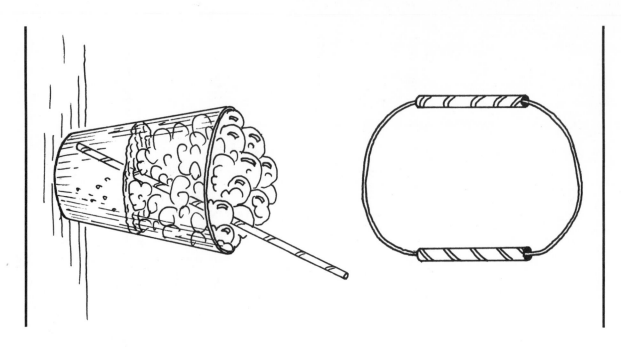

- Give the guests plastic berry baskets and have them dip the baskets into the bubble solution. Gently lift the baskets out of the solution and wave them through the air. Many bubbles will flow from the baskets.

- For each guest, fill an empty juice can halfway with the bubble solution. Pass out the bubble pipes and let the children experiment.

- Give two 6" pieces of plastic straws and a 30" piece of string to each guest. Each child threads the string through both straws and ties the string ends into a knot. Slip the knot inside one of the straws. Position the straws so they are parallel. Hold the straws and dip the bubble stretcher into the bubble solution. Lift it out of the solution carefully. A large bubble will stretch across the center. The bubble will twist and change color as the straws are moved.

Bubble Pictures
Fill four cups halfway with bubble solution. Add a different color food coloring to each cup. Give each guest a plastic straw and a piece of manilla paper or typing paper. The child blows through the straw into the solution in one of the cups, making bubbles at the top. The guest then lays the paper on the bubbles. As the bubbles pop they will leave a pale design. Have the child move the straw to a different color solution and repeat. The final pictures will contain all four colors, and each design will be unique. The children will want to make several of these beautiful pictures.

Bubble Gum Blowing Contest
Pass out the sugarless bubblegum and see who can blow the biggest bubble.

Dancing Moth Balls
Add one tablespoon white vinegar to a glass of water. Be sure to use a clear glass. Add 1/2 teaspoon baking soda and drop in four napthalene mothballs. Observe the action that takes place. The bubbles generate enough power to move the mothballs.

Doll Tea Party
Invite one friend and a doll or stuffed animal to a tea party. The child should do most of the preparations. If she or he has a little table and chair set and a small tea set, all the better. A fancy tablecloth and two or three flowers are musts. The host child can make divine party hats from paper plates, curly ribbon and crepe paper before the party or the children can make them together before lunch is served.

Menu:
Dainty sandwiches (cut crusts from bread and cut each sandwich into four small triangles or cut into fancy shapes with small cookie cutters.)
A bunch of green grapes or melon balls
Cups of tea or apple juice
Small cookies or miniature cupcakes
After lunch provide dress-up clothes and time and space to pretend.

Everyone Helps Party

Save used wrapping paper for a spur-of-the-moment, do-it-as-a-group party. Early in the day wrap a mystery package in a number of layers, each containing a special assignment and the materials needed to complete the task. In the evening gather the family in the room where the party will take place. Ask one family member to unwrap the first layer and complete the first task, then pass the package to the next person to complete the next task and so on.

Package items and instructions could include some of the following but can be expanded to include ideas and activities that will create a festive atmosphere and are particularly appropriate to your family.

- A few balloons and a roll of tape to hang them.
- A roll of crepe paper and tape.
- Matches to light the candles in the room.
- A box of mints or other favorite family treat.
- Party hats or paper plates, yarn, curly ribbon, construction paper and glue to make hats.
- Songsheets and instructions to lead the family in singing two or three songs.
- A new card game, board game, book, or tape — something everyone can share right away.
- A small box for a game of animal charades. Fill the box with pictures of animals. Each player draws a picture from the box and mimes the animal while the others guess what animal he or she is.
- Construction paper, scissors, glue, crayons or markers for everyone to make cards for each other or for another family.
- As a final item, party napkins to pass out to each family member. Serve frosted cupcakes and bowls of ice cream. Pass a tray of do-it-yourself decorations: small bowls of chocolate chips, colored sugar sprinkles, raisins, grated coconut, miniature marshmallows, chopped nuts, and whipped cream.

Night Hike

Suprise everyone with an invitation for a night hike on a beautiful starry night. A walk to the neighborhood park to gaze at the constellations or a late night adventure in the backyard can be enchanting. For a better view of the stars, drive away from the city lights. Take along a snack of star-shaped sugar cookies, a thermos of hot chocolate and cups. Point out favorite star groups such as the Big Dipper and Little Dipper and any planets that are visible. Most newspapers list planets and major constellations for those who are new at star gazing. Be very quiet and listen to the night sounds.

Sidewalk Surprise

Colored chalk, homemade beanbags and a sidewalk sound ordinary but they can transform an ordinary summer afternoon into a memorable occasion. The day before the party, invite two or three friends to meet on your sidewalk for something special to do.

Get ready for the party by sewing two 5 x 8" pieces of sturdy fabric together on three sides to make one pouch for each child. As the children arrive, give them each a pouch and have them write their names on the pouches with indelible marker. Then have the children fill the pouches with dried beans, rice or popping corn. Leave some room at the top so the contents can move around. Have double-threaded needles ready for the children to sew closed the open end of the pouches to complete the beanbags. Younger children will need help with the sewing. Instead of sewing, you can tie the fourth side closed with colored yarn. Each child will have a beanbag for the day's activities and to take home. This is a good activity for sitting in the grass because you don't have to worry about spilled stuffings. Give each child a wrapped favor of colored chalk - a box or several pieces tied together with yarn.

Use the chalk and the beanbags for several sidewalk games.

- Draw a hopscotch diagram.
- Have the guests draw lines to jump over.
- Ask the guests to draw lines to mark the start and finish for movements called out by an adult such as "Skip between the lines," "Hop between the lines," "Run between the lines," or "Duck-walk between the lines."
- Have the children throw beanbags to hit targets they've drawn.
- Draw two lines on the sidewalk for each pair of children. One child stands behind each line and they toss the beanbags to each other. Line spacing can be adjusted by the children as they choose to make the toss more or less challenging.

• Give the children scoops made from plastic milk bottles to make a game of beanbag catch more interesting.

After the guests have played the sidewalk games for a while, invite them to make chalk pictures on the sidewalk. Assign a square or two to each child for his or her artwork.

Serve Sunshine Pops after admiring each others' artwork.

Sunshine Pops

4 oranges
2 lemons
2 bananas
1/2 cup sugar
2 cups water

1. *Mix* the sugar and water in a saucepan and cook over medium heat.
2. *Remove* from the heat and let cool for 15 minutes.
3. *Squeeze* the juice from the fruit. Mash the bananas with a fork.
4. *Add* the citrus juice to the mashed bananas and mix well.
5. *Add* the sugar-water mixture and mix well.
6. *Pour* 1/3 cup of the mixture into small paper cups and place in the freezer.
7. *After 30 minutes insert* a popsicle stick or small plastic spoon into the middle of each cup and return to the freezer. Freeze at least 3 hours.
   Makes 6 popsicles.

Index

Games—Outdoor

Celebration Memories

Child's Name _____ Age _____

Date of Party _____

Theme Used _____

Comments and Special Memories _____

_____

_____

_____

Child's Name _____ Age _____

Date of Party _____

Theme Used _____

Comments and Special Memories _____

_____

_____

_____

Child's Name _____ Age _____

Date of Party _____

Theme Used _____

Comments and Special Memories _____

_____

_____

_____

Child's Name _____ Age _____

Date of Party _____

Theme Used _____

Comments and Special Memories _____

_____

_____

Child's Name _____ Age _____

Date of Party _____

Theme Used _____

Comments and Special Memories _____

_____

_____

Child's Name _____

Date of Party _____ Age _____

Theme Used _____

Comments and Special Memories _____

_____

_____

Child's Name _____

Date of Party _____ Age _____

Theme Used _____

Comments and Special Memories _____

_____

_____

Child's Name _____

Date of Party _____ Age _____

Theme Used _____

Comments and Special Memories _____

_____

_____

Child's Name _____

Date of Party _____ Age _____

Theme Used _____

Comments and Special Memories _____

_____

_____

Celebrate!

me and address (please print or type)
ck or money order for $9.95 per copy.
r the first book and .50 for each additional copy.

Rainbow Publishing Co.
First United Church
Nursery School

848 W. Lake Street
Oak Park, IL 60301